JUST SAY
"FUCK IT
THANK YOU"
A Book on Gratitude,
for Life's Challenges

Introduction

In a world that often feels like it's spinning too fast, where demands on our time and energy can leave us feeling depleted and disconnected, the power of two simple words can transform our entire outlook on life. These words are not magical incantations nor are they secret codes to an ancient wisdom. They are, however, gateways to a profound shift in perspective: from a place of resistance to one of acceptance and gratitude.

"f*ck It" – a phrase so many of us have whispered under our breath or screamed into our pillows in moments of frustration, defeat, or despair. It's the verbal manifestation of hitting a wall, of feeling so overwhelmed by the complexities and challenges of life that giving up seems like the only option. But what if, in these moments of utter defeat, we chose a different path? What if we said, "Thank You" instead?

"Thank You" doesn't negate the hardships or pretend the obstacles don't exist. Instead, it offers a powerful reframe – a way to acknowledge the struggle while opening ourselves up to the possibility of growth, learning, and connection. It's about recognizing the value in every experience, good or bad, and finding the strength to move forward with gratitude and resilience.

This book is an invitation to embark on a journey of transformation. It's about learning to let go of what doesn't serve us and embracing what does with open hearts and minds. It's about discovering the profound impact of gratitude on our relationships, our self-perception, and our approach to life's inevitable ups and downs. Through personal stories, practical advice, and interactive exercises, "Just Say f*ck It Thank You" aims to guide you toward a more fulfilling, authentic, and empowered existence.

Authors Note

Dear Reader,

As you hold this book in your hands, I want to thank you. Thank you for being open to exploring the pages within, for being curious about the power of gratitude, and for taking the first step on what I hope will be a transformative journey for you.

*This book was born out of my own moments of saying "f*ck It" – out of frustration, exhaustion, and sometimes despair. I've been where you might find yourself now: at a crossroads, wondering if there's a different, perhaps better, way to navigate life's challenges. Through my own journey of self-discovery, I've learned that the most powerful tool we have is our perspective. Changing "f*ck It" to "Thank You" has been a pivotal shift in my life, and it is my deepest hope that by sharing this shift with you, you too can find a path to deeper fulfillment and joy.*

As you embark on this journey, remember that transformation is not a destination but a process. There will be setbacks and challenges, but there will also be victories and moments of profound joy. My hope is that "Just Say Thank You" serves as a companion and guide, offering you light during the dark times and amplifying your joy during the good ones.

Sasha M Myrom

Part 1
The Journey to Self Discovery

CHAPTER 1:
UNDERSTANDING YOURSELF

In the mosaic of life, each piece represents a part of us —our experiences, choices, beliefs, and relationships. How we fit these pieces together depends significantly on our understanding of ourselves. This foundational knowledge is not just a pillar of personal development; it is the bedrock upon which happiness and fulfilling relationships are built. It's about peeling back the layers to reveal our true selves, not who we think we should be or who others expect us to be.

Self-understanding goes beyond mere introspection. It involves a deep dive into our values, motivations, fears, and desires. It's about recognizing our strengths and acknowledging our weaknesses. This journey of self-discovery is crucial for several reasons. Firstly, it empowers us to make choices that are in alignment with our true selves, leading to a more authentic and fulfilling life. When we understand what truly matters to us, we can pursue goals and relationships that resonate with our core values, rather than being swayed by external expectations or societal pressures.

Secondly, self-understanding is the foundation of emotional intelligence. It enhances our capacity for empathy, allowing us to connect with others on a deeper level. Genuine connections are formed when we see and accept our own vulnerabilities, as this openness invites others to share their true selves with us. This mutual vulnerability is the soil from which trust and intimacy grow, strengthening the bonds we share with those around us.

Lastly, knowing ourselves improves our resilience. Life is unpredictable, filled with challenges and setbacks. A deep understanding of our inner world equips us with the tools to navigate these challenges with grace and adaptability. When we know our triggers and emotional responses, we can manage stress and conflict more effectively, maintaining our equilibrium in the face of adversity. We can effectively assess a situation and transform the emotional reaction of "f*ck it" into a valuable opportunity for growth, saying "Thank you" instead.

Unpacking Your Personal History

To understand ourselves deeply, it's essential to unpack this history, examining the patterns and pivotal events that have influenced our beliefs, behaviors, and perspectives. This exploration is not about dwelling in the past but about understanding its impact on the present and how it can inform our journey toward a more authentic future. As you delve into your personal history, approach yourself with compassion and curiosity, recognizing that every experience has contributed to the rich, complex person you are today.

<u>Exercises to Explore Personal History</u>

1. Timeline of Life Events

> Create a timeline of your life, marking significant events, relationships, and periods. Include both challenging and joyful times.

> Reflect on each event: What did you learn? How did it influence your view of yourself, others, or the world?

2. Influential People Map

> Draw a map that centers on you and branches out to the people who have significantly influenced your life (family, friends, teachers, etc.).

> Next to each name, note how they've impacted you. What beliefs or behaviors do you attribute to their influence? These impacts can range from positive to negative. This process of reflection helps us refine our preferences and promotes growth in aligning more closely with our true desires.

3. Patterns in Relationships

> List the significant relationships in your life, noting

the qualities that attracted you to these individuals and the dynamics that played out.

➢ Look for patterns: Are there recurring themes or behaviors in these relationships? What might these patterns reveal about your needs or fears?

Reflection Questions

1. How has your upbringing shaped your beliefs about love, success, and happiness?

Consider the messages you received from family, culture, and society about what it means to be successful, loved, or happy. How have these messages influenced your life choices?

2. What pivotal moments have defined your outlook on life?

Identify moments that felt like turning points in your understanding of yourself or the world. How did these moments change your direction or perspective?

3. How do past relationships influence your current ones?

Reflect on the impact of significant past relationships on how you relate to others now. Are there fears, expectations, or behaviors that you carry into new relationships?

4. What beliefs or behaviors do you want to change, and which do you want to keep?

Based on your reflections, identify which aspects of your personal history you see as valuable and which you might want to reconsider or let go of.

Identifying Your Core Values

Understanding your core values and how they influence your life can provide profound insights into your personal and interpersonal world; they can help people understand the difference between what is important to them and what might be the byproduct of societal or external pressures. Identifying and defining your core values allows you to live more authentically, make decisions that align with your true self, and build deeper, more meaningful relationships. As you continue to grow and evolve, your understanding of your core values may shift. Regular reflection on these values ensures that your actions and decisions remain aligned with who you are at your core.

<u>Guidance on Identifying and Defining Core Values</u>

Understanding Core Values

➤ Begin by understanding what core values are: intrinsic beliefs that represent your highest priorities, deeply held beliefs, and fundamental driving forces.

➤ Recognize that core values are personal. They are your compass in life, guiding you towards decisions and actions that fulfill you.

Identifying Your Core Values

➤ Reflect on moments when you felt happiest or most proud. What were you doing? Who were you with? These moments can reveal what you value most.

➤ Consider the opposite: Reflect on times you were unhappy or disappointed in yourself. Often, these moments conflict with our core values.

Defining Your Core Values

➤ From your reflections, list potential values that resonate with you. Don't limit yourself at this stage; list everything that feels significant.

➤ Once you have a broad list, narrow it down. Aim for 5-10 core values that deeply resonate with you. Definitions are crucial; define each value in terms that are meaningful and specific to you.

Activities to Prioritize Your Values and Understand Their Influence

Activity 1: The Value Sort

➤ Write each of your identified core values on separate pieces of paper.

➤ Sort these values into order of importance to you.
   * *This process can be challenging but illuminating. It requires you to deeply consider what values are truly paramount.*

➤ Reflect on why your top values are so important to you. How do they shape your daily life, decisions, and interactions with others?

Activity 2: The Daily Decision Diary

➤ For one week, keep a diary of your decisions, noting which core values influenced these decisions.

➤ At the end of the week, review your diary. You'll likely see patterns that highlight how your core values guide your behavior and decision-making process.

Activity 3: Values in Relationships

➤ Reflect on your key relationships and how your core values align or misalign with those of the people you're closest to.

➤ This activity can help you understand the dynamics

of your relationships and why certain relationships feel more fulfilling or challenging.

Acknowledging Your
Needs and Desires

By acknowledging and understanding your needs and desires, you gain valuable insights into what drives you and how you can achieve personal fulfillment. This clarity can also improve your relationships, as it allows for transparent communication of what you require and desire from your partners, friends, and family. While needs are essentials for your well-being and survival, desires are your wants that add joy, satisfaction, and richness to life. Both play significant roles in shaping your choices, actions, and interactions with others.*

<u>Techniques for Distinguishing Between Needs and Desires</u>

1. The Hierarchy Approach

   Use Maslow's Hierarchy of Needs as a starting point to categorize your needs from physiological (most basic) to self-actualization (most complex).
   Anything that falls outside these categories can often be considered a desire, enhancing your life's quality but not essential for well-being.

2. The Urgency Test

   Ask yourself, "Can I live without this?" If something is non-negotiable for your mental, physical, or emotional health, it's likely a need. If it's something you aspire to have because it brings you happiness or satisfaction, it's a desire.

3. The Long-term vs. Short-term Fulfillment

   Needs often have a long-term impact on your fulfillment and well-being, while desires may provide short-term pleasure or satisfaction. Distinguishing between the two can help in prioritizing them effectively.

Prompts to Articulate Your Needs and Desires

Emotional Needs

➢ What makes you feel loved and supported?

➢ Reflect on a time you felt emotionally fulfilled. What need was being met?

Physical Needs

➢ Consider your basic needs for food, shelter, and health. Are there specific aspects of these needs that are particularly important to you (e.g., dietary requirements, a safe and peaceful living environment)?

Intellectual Needs

➢ What stimulates your mind and keeps you engaged?

➢ Think about activities that challenge you intellectually. How often are these needs met?

Spiritual Needs

➢ Reflect on what gives your life meaning and purpose. This could be religion, but it can also include connection with nature, art, or community.

➢ How do you nourish your spirit, and what practices are essential for your inner peace?

Desires

➢ List the things you want in life that bring you joy, satisfaction, or pleasure. These can range from career aspirations to hobbies and leisure activities.

➢ How do these desires complement your needs, and how do you balance pursuing them with meeting your needs?

The Role of Self-Esteem
in Self-Understanding

Self-esteem is the lens through which we view ourselves and our place in the world. It profoundly impacts our self-perception, the quality of our relationships, and our ability to navigate life's challenges.

The Impact of Self-Esteem on Self-Perception and Relationships

Self-Perception:

➤ High self-esteem encourages a realistic and positive view of oneself, acknowledging strengths and accepting weaknesses without undue self-criticism.

➤ Low self-esteem often leads to distorted self-perception, where one's flaws are magnified, and strengths are minimized or ignored.

Relationships:

➤ A positive self-image allows for healthier relationships based on mutual respect and genuine connection, as individuals with high self-esteem are more likely to establish boundaries and communicate their needs effectively.

➤ Low self-esteem can contribute to dysfunctional relationship patterns, including dependency, fear of abandonment, or tolerating mistreatment due to a belief that one is undeserving of better.

Strategies for Building a Positive Self-Image

Identify and Challenge Negative Beliefs:

➢ Write down negative beliefs you hold about yourself. Question their validity and challenge them with evidence of your capabilities and worth.

Practice Positive Affirmations:

➢ Create affirmations that counteract your critical thoughts and reflect your values and strengths. Repeat these daily to reinforce a positive self-view.

Set Realistic Goals:

➢ Setting and achieving realistic goals, even small ones, can significantly boost your self-esteem by proving your ability to accomplish tasks and make positive changes.

➢ Exercises to Promote Self-Compassion and Acceptance

The Mirror Exercise:

➢ Stand in front of a mirror, look into your eyes, and compliment yourself. Focus on qualities you admire about yourself, both physical and character strengths. It may feel awkward initially, but it's a powerful exercise in self-acceptance.

Self-Compassion Break:

➢ Whenever you notice self-criticism or harsh self-judgment, pause for a self-compassion break. Speak to yourself as you would to a dear friend facing the same issue, with kindness and understanding.

Gratitude Journaling for Self-Acceptance:

➢ Keep a gratitude journal focused on aspects of yourself you're thankful for. This could include talents, moments of resilience, ways you've helped others, or simply parts of your character that make you unique.

The Three-Column Technique:

➤   Create three columns on a piece of paper. First, write down a negative self-thought. Second, note the emotions and behaviors that thought evokes. Third, challenge the negative thought with a more balanced, compassionate perspective.

The Power of Self-Reflection

Self-reflection is a powerful tool, offering a path to deeper understanding, personal growth, and mindful living. We can cultivate a heightened awareness of our thoughts, feelings, and behaviors with some of the practices discussed below. Self-reflection is a personal journey unique to each individual. Remember, the goal is not perfection but progress toward a more conscious and fulfilling life.

Introduction to Self-Reflection Practices

Journaling: Writing down your thoughts, feelings, and experiences on a regular basis. It provides a private, unfiltered space to explore your inner world, identify patterns in your thoughts and behaviors, and clarify your desires and goals.

> *Benefits:* Journaling enhances self-awareness, emotional intelligence, and problem-solving skills. It can also serve as a therapeutic tool for processing emotions and experiences.

Meditation: Focusing your mind on a particular object, thought, or activity to achieve a mentally clear and emotionally calm state.

> *Benefits:* Regular meditation reduces stress, improves concentration, and promotes a greater sense of peace and well-being. It also fosters a deeper connection with oneself.

Mindfulness: Being fully present and engaged in the moment, aware of your thoughts and feelings without distraction or judgment.

> *Benefits:* Practicing mindfulness enhances emotional regulation, reduces negative thinking, and increases tolerance for difficult emotions. It encourages a compassionate, non-judgmental approach to self-reflection.

Implementing a Regular Self-Reflection Routine

Step 1: Choose Your Practice(s)

Consider your lifestyle, preferences, and goals. You may be drawn to one practice over others or find a combination beneficial. Start with what feels most accessible and appealing to you.

Step 2: Set a Regular Time and Place

Consistency is key. Choose a time and place where you can engage in your self-reflection practice without interruptions. Whether it's journaling each morning, meditating before bed, or practicing mindfulness during your daily walk, establish a routine that fits your schedule.

Step 3: Start Small

Begin with short periods of practice (e.g., five minutes of meditation or journaling) and gradually increase the duration as it becomes a natural part of your routine.

Step 4: Make it a Habit

Incorporate your chosen practice(s) into your daily routine. Setting reminders or linking your practice to an existing habit (e.g., after brushing your teeth) can help reinforce this new habit.

Step 5: Reflect on Your Practice

Periodically, take time to reflect on how your self-reflection practice is impacting your life. Consider what insights you've gained, any changes in your self-awareness or well-being, and adjustments you might want to make to your practice.

Step 6: Be Patient and Kind to Yourself

Developing a new habit takes time and patience. Approach your self-reflection practice with kindness and curiosity, rather than judgment or strict expectations.

Reflection and Action Steps

It's important to pause and reflect on the key takeaways that can guide us on journey of self-discovery that lays the foundation for the transformative power of saying "Thank You" instead of "f*ck It."

Summary of Key Takeaways

Self-Understanding is the Foundation: Recognizing and embracing your unique experiences, values, and desires is crucial for personal growth and fulfilling relationships.

The Power of Personal History: Your past experiences shape your present beliefs and behaviors. Reflecting on these can provide valuable insights into your character and motivations.

Identifying Core Values: Understanding your core values is essential for making decisions that align with your true self.

Acknowledging Needs and Desires: Distinguishing between your needs and desires helps clarify what truly matters to you, guiding your path to fulfillment.

The Role of Self-Esteem: A healthy self-esteem is vital for a positive self-perception and healthy relationships. It's something to nurture and protect.

Self-Reflection Practices: Engaging in practices like journaling, meditation, and mindfulness can enhance self-awareness and emotional clarity.

Suggested Action Steps

1. Create a Personal History Timeline:

Set aside time to map out significant life events and relationships. Reflect on how these have shaped your beliefs and behaviors.

2. Define Your Core Values:

Write down a list of values that resonate with you. Narrow them down to your top 5-10 and define what they mean to you personally.

3. Needs vs. Desires Exercise:

Make two lists, one for your needs and one for your desires. Reflect on how each item affects your life choices and relationships.

4. Daily Self-Esteem Boost:

Practice positive affirmations every morning or engage in the mirror exercise to nurture your self-esteem.

5. Implement a Self-Reflection Routine:

Choose a self-reflection practice (journaling, meditation, or mindfulness) and incorporate it into your daily routine, even if just for a few minutes each day.

6. Explore Your Self-Perception:

Regularly ask yourself, "How do I see myself?" and "How do others see me?" Compare these perceptions and consider areas for growth or reassessment.

7. Practice Gratitude:

End each day by writing down three things you are grateful for about yourself. These could be qualities, achievements, or moments of resilience.

Conclusion: Embracing Your Unique Self

It's vital to remember that understanding yourself is a dynamic and ongoing process. The path to self-awareness is not linear and it offers endless opportunities for growth, learning, and deeper connections. Embracing your unique self—flaws, strengths, quirks, and all—is the cornerstone of living authentically and fostering relationships that are truly fulfilling. In a world that often pressures us to conform, standing firm in who you are is an act of bravery. Remember, there is no one else with your combination of thoughts, experiences, passions, and dreams. Celebrating your uniqueness isn't just about acknowledging your strengths but also embracing your vulnerabilities and imperfections. These aspects of your identity are not weaknesses; they are facets of your humanity that connect you to others in meaningful ways.

As you grow and evolve, so too will your understanding of yourself. Each experience, challenge, and relationship offers new insights into who you are and what you value. This journey is not about reaching a final destination where you know everything there is to know about yourself. Rather, it's about remaining open to learning and evolving, allowing your self-perception to expand and deepen over time. It's an invitation to continually shape and refine who you are and who you wish to become. In embracing your unique self and viewing self-understanding as an evolving process, you open the door to a life of authenticity, fulfillment, and profound connection. May this journey bring you closer to your true self, enriching your life and the lives of those you share it with.

CHAPTER 2: THE LANGUAGE OF SELF-LOVE

The power of this self-talk is immense, shaping not only how we view ourselves but also how we interact within our communities.

Our self-talk is a reflection of our innermost beliefs about who we are. When this dialogue is positive, it reinforces a sense of self-worth and competence, encouraging us to tackle challenges with confidence. Positive self-talk can be a wellspring of motivation, driving us forward with hope and resilience. It can elevate our mood, reduce our stress, and enhance our ability to cope with life's inevitable challenges. Conversely, negative self-talk can trap us in a cycle of self-doubt and limitation, convincing us of our inadequacies and hindering our potential for growth. Negative self-talk can be a significant source of anxiety and depression, coloring our experiences with pessimism and fear, and limiting our capacity to achieve our fullest potential.

Understanding the nature of our self-talk is the first step towards harnessing its power to foster a healthier, more empowered self-perception. The impact of self-talk extends beyond transient emotions and behaviors, influencing our psychological health and overall quality of life. Engaging in a pattern of negative self-talk can reinforce harmful beliefs and attitudes, contributing to a distorted self-image and impaired emotional well-being. Positive self-talk, however, can be a powerful tool for psychological resilience, promoting mental health and fostering an adaptive, optimistic outlook on life.

As we explore our internal dialogue, it becomes clear that the nature of our self-talk is not merely a matter of positive versus negative; it is a reflection of our relationship with ourselves. By cultivating awareness of our self-talk and intentionally shifting towards more positive, supportive dialogue, we can transform our relationship with ourselves and, consequently, with the world around us.

Recognizing Negative
Self-Talk

Negative self-talk can be a formidable barrier to personal growth and happiness, often operating just below the surface of our conscious awareness. Recognizing negative self-talk is a crucial first step in changing the narrative. By becoming more aware of these patterns and understanding their triggers, you can begin to dismantle the power they hold over you. Through mindfulness, journaling, and critical examination, you can start to replace your critical inner voice with a more compassionate and empowering one.

<u>Techniques for Becoming More Aware of Negative Self-Talk</u>

1. Mindfulness Practice:

   Begin by cultivating mindfulness, the practice of being present and fully engaged with the moment without judgment. Mindfulness can help you become more aware of your thoughts, including the automatic negative messages that may flow beneath your conscious awareness.

2. Journaling:

   Keeping a thought diary can be an effective way to track your self-talk. For one week, write down any negative or critical thoughts that come to mind throughout your day. Note the situation, your feelings at the time, and the outcome of the situation. This can help you identify patterns in your negative self-talk.

3. Trigger Identification:

   Certain situations may trigger negative self-talk more than others. Pay attention to when your inner critic is most vocal. Is it during work, social interactions, or when you're alone? Identifying triggers can help you anticipate and manage negative self-talk.

Examples of Common Negative Narratives
- o Self-Doubt: *"I can't do this. I'm not good enough."*
- o Catastrophizing: *"If I fail this, everything will fall apart."*
- o Overgeneralization: *"I messed up this time. I always mess things up."*
- o Personalization: *"This happened because I did something wrong."*

Activities to Identify and Understand Your Critical Inner Voice

Activity 1: The Two-Column Technique

Create a two-column chart in your journal. In the left column, write down instances of negative self-talk you've noticed. In the right column, challenge these thoughts with evidence or a more positive perspective. This activity encourages critical thinking about the validity of your negative self-talk.

Activity 2: The Role of the Observer

For a day, pretend you are an observer of your own thoughts. Every time you notice a negative thought, imagine you're a friend listening in. How would you respond to a friend who spoke about themselves that way? This can help you cultivate compassion towards yourself.

Activity 3: Identifying Patterns

Using your thought diary, look for patterns in your negative self-talk. Are there specific themes or words that recur? Understanding these patterns can make them more recognizable in the future, allowing you to actively counter them.

Challenges to Self-Love

Overcoming the challenges to self-love requires a conscious effort to recognize and resist the external and internal influences that feed self-criticism. These barriers often manifest as deep-seated beliefs and attitudes that significantly hinder our ability to love and accept ourselves. This journey is not about achieving perfection but about embracing oneself, flaws and all, with kindness and compassion.

<u>Societal and Cultural Influences</u>

- *Societal Expectations:* Society often imposes strict standards regarding success, beauty, behavior, and values. These standards can create an environment where individuals feel pressured to conform, leading to feelings of inadequacy when they fail to meet these expectations.

- *Cultural Norms:* Cultural backgrounds influence perceptions of self-worth and identity. In some cultures, collective values may overshadow individuality, making self-expression and self-acceptance challenging. Conversely, cultures that highly value individual achievement may lead to an excessive focus on competition and personal success, fostering self-criticism over perceived failures.

- *Media Representation:* Media plays a significant role in shaping our ideals of perfection. Constant exposure to idealized images and narratives can distort our self-image and exacerbate feelings of not being good enough.

<u>Personal Influences</u>

- *Family Dynamics:* Early family environments and dynamics significantly impact our self-esteem and self-perception. Messages received from family members about worth, capability, and appearance can deeply influence how we view ourselves into adulthood.

➤ *Past Traumas:* Experiences of trauma, including bullying, abuse, or neglect, can leave lasting scars on self-esteem. These experiences may foster a critical inner voice that undermines self-love and acceptance.

➤ *Comparison and Competition:* The tendency to compare oneself to others, especially in the age of social media, can be a profound source of self-criticism and discontent. This comparison often overlooks the unique challenges and circumstances of each individual's life.

<u>Reflections on Personal Experiences and Beliefs</u>

➤ *Identifying Root Causes:* Reflect on the origins of your self-critical thoughts. Can you trace them back to specific societal messages, cultural pressures, or personal experiences? Acknowledging these sources can be the first step in challenging and changing them.

➤ *Challenging Negative Beliefs:* Consider the beliefs that contribute to your self-criticism. Are they truly your own, or have they been internalized from external influences? Questioning the validity and origin of these beliefs can help diminish their power over you.

➤ *Reframing Experiences:* Reflect on how past challenges have contributed to your growth and resilience. Viewing difficult experiences through the lens of growth, rather than as evidence of inadequacy, can foster a more compassionate self-view.

Shifting Towards Positive Self-Talk

By actively challenging negative self-talk and cultivating a practice of personalized affirmations, you can significantly shift the way you view yourself and engage with the world. This shift not only enhances your emotional well-being but also empowers you to approach life with confidence and resilience. This transformation doesn't happen overnight, but with persistence and patience, you will begin to notice a profound change in your self-perception and emotional resilience.

<u>Strategies for Challenging Negative Self-Talk</u>

1. Awareness and Identification:

    The first step is becoming aware of when and how you engage in negative self-talk. Identify specific instances and the triggers that prompt this critical inner dialogue.

2. Question and Challenge:

    Once identified, question the accuracy and helpfulness of these negative thoughts. Are they based on facts or distorted perceptions? Challenge these thoughts by looking for evidence that contradicts them.

3. Cognitive Restructuring:

    This involves replacing negative thoughts with more balanced and realistic ones. Instead of thinking, "I always fail," reframe it to, "I have had setbacks, but I also have successes."

4. Practice Self-Compassion:

    Treat yourself with the same kindness and understanding you would offer a friend. Acknowledge that everyone has flaws and makes mistakes, and these do not define your worth.

<u>Creating Personalized Affirmations</u>

Step 1: Reflect on Your Values and Goals

Consider what is genuinely important to you and what you aim to achieve or embody. Your affirmations should resonate with your core values and aspirations.

Step 2: Identify Areas for Growth

Focus on aspects of yourself or your life you wish to improve or reinforce. This could relate to your confidence, resilience, relationships, or any other personal growth area.

Step 3: Craft Your Affirmation

Write affirmations that are positive, in the present tense, and assert what you wish to be true. For example, "I am capable of overcoming challenges," or "I am worthy of love and respect."

Step 4: Personalize Your Language

Use language that feels natural and compelling to you. Affirmations should feel like a genuine expression of your aspirations and self-view.

Step 5: Integrate Affirmations into Your Daily Routine

Find moments throughout your day to repeat your affirmations, such as in the morning, during a break, or before bed. You can say them out loud, write them down, or even display them where you'll regularly see them.

Step 6: Practice Regularly

Like any habit, the practice of affirmations becomes more effective over time. Consistency is key to embedding these positive messages in your subconscious.

The Role of Affirmations in Self-Love

Practicing self-compassion is an ongoing journey, not a one-time achievement. It requires patience, repetition, and a willingness to confront and soften self-critical tendencies. By incorporating these exercises into your daily routine, you can strengthen your self-compassion muscle, leading to greater emotional resilience, a kinder self-dialogue, and a deeper capacity for self-love. Remember, the relationship you have with yourself sets the tone for every other relationship in your life. Cultivating self-compassion is, therefore, not just an act of kindness towards yourself but a foundation for healthier, more fulfilling interactions with others.

How Affirmations Work

Affirmations work by leveraging the brain's plasticity, its ability to change and adapt in response to repeated thoughts and behaviors. By consistently practicing positive affirmations, you can begin to alter the neural pathways that govern your thoughts and feelings, gradually shifting from a critical or negative mindset to one that is more affirming and optimistic.

This process helps in reducing stress, improving your outlook on life, and increasing your self-esteem.

Benefits of Affirmations in Self-Love

Boosts Self-Esteem: Regularly affirming your worth and capabilities helps reinforce your confidence and self-belief.

Enhances Positive Thinking: Affirmations can shift your focus from dwelling on perceived failures or inadequacies to recognizing your strengths and potential.

Promotes Emotional Resilience: By cultivating a positive self-image, affirmations help you navigate challenges and setbacks with greater ease and optimism.

Improves Mental Health: Engaging in positive self-talk through affirmations can decrease symptoms of anxiety and depression, contributing to overall well-being.

<u>Practical Tips for Integrating Affirmations into Daily Routines</u>

1. Morning Affirmation Ritual:

Start your day by reciting affirmations. This could be while you're still in bed, during your morning skincare routine, or while preparing breakfast. Choose affirmations that inspire you for the day ahead, such as *"Today, I choose joy and gratitude."*

2. Affirmation Alarms:

Set multiple alarms throughout the day with different affirmations as the label. Each time an alarm goes off, take a moment to repeat the affirmation to yourself. This ensures that you're regularly reminded to engage in positive self-talk.

3. Visual Affirmation Reminders:

Place sticky notes with your favorite affirmations in areas where you'll see them often—your bathroom mirror, computer monitor, or the dashboard of your car. These visual cues can serve as constant reminders to maintain a positive mindset.

4. Reflective Affirmation Practice:

In the evening, reflect on your day and acknowledge any successes or moments of joy. Then, recite affirmations that reinforce these positive experiences, such as *"I am proud of myself for my achievements today."*

5. Affirmation Journaling:

Dedicate a section of your journal to affirmations. Write down new affirmations that resonate with your experiences or goals. Regularly reviewing and writing affirmations can deepen their impact on your subconscious.

Practicing Self-Compassion

Self-compassion is a fundamental aspect of self-love, emphasizing kindness towards oneself, especially in times of failure or disappointment. This concept involves treating yourself with the same care and understanding you would offer to a good friend in distress. It is rooted in the recognition that imperfection and struggle are part of the shared human experience.

<u>Understanding Self-Compassion- the three main components</u>

Self - Kindness vs. Self Judgement:

Treating yourself with kindness rather than harsh criticism when you are suffering or notice something you dislike about yourself.

Common Humanity vs. Isolation:

Recognizing that suffering and personal inadequacy are part of the shared human experiance - something that we all go through rather than something that happens to "me" alone.

Mindfulness vs Over-Identification:

Observing your negative emotions with openness and clarity, so you are neither ignoring or exaggerating them.

<u>Exercises to Develop Self-Compassion</u>

The Self-Compassion Break

> Whenever you encounter a difficult situation or start to feel overwhelmed by negative emotions, take a self-compassion break. Pause for a moment, place a hand over your heart, and acknowledge your suffering with a simple statement like, *"This is really hard right now."* Remind yourself of the common human experience of suffering, and offer yourself some kind words of support, such as,

"May I give myself the compassion I need."

Writing a Letter to Yourself

Write a letter to yourself from the perspective of a compassionate friend. Address a specific situation that caused you pain or disappointment. In the letter, express understanding, kindness, and a recognition of your common humanity. This exercise helps you to externalize self-compassion and practice directing it towards yourself.

The Compassionate Observer Meditation

Spend a few minutes each day practicing mindfulness meditation focused on developing self-compassion. Begin by focusing on your breath to ground yourself in the present moment. Then, bring to mind a situation that is causing you distress. Observe the emotions that arise without judgment, offering yourself understanding and kindness. Use phrases like, *"It's okay to feel this way,"* or, *"I am here for myself,"* to cultivate a compassionate inner voice.

Cultivating Gratitude for Yourself

At the end of each day, write down three things you appreciate about yourself. These can be qualities, actions you took that day, or simply the fact that you navigated another day's challenges. This practice helps shift the focus from self-criticism to appreciation and gratitude for oneself.

Building a Self-Love Ritual

By setting aside specific times for self-love practices, you create structured opportunities to nurture your relationship with yourself. What works for you may change over time as you grow and your needs shift. The key is to remain committed to this practice, making it a non-negotiable part of your routine. By doing so, you reinforce the importance of your well-being and the value of dedicating time to nurture your relationship with yourself.

<u>Designing Your Self-Love Ritual</u>

Daily Affirmations:

Begin your day with affirmations that focus on self-acceptance, strength, and the acknowledgment of your worth. Choose affirmations that resonate with your personal journey and repeat them each morning to set a positive tone for the day.

Gratitude Journaling:

Dedicate a few minutes each evening to write down three things you are grateful for about yourself. These could be qualities you appreciate, achievements of the day, or simply acts of kindness you offered to yourself or others.

Weekly Self-Reflection:

Set aside time each week to reflect on your experiences, emotions, and growth. Use this time to assess your needs, celebrate your progress, and set intentions for the coming week.

Mindful Movement:

Incorporate a form of physical activity that you enjoy and that promotes mindfulness, such as yoga, dancing, or walking in nature. Engage in this activity regularly as a celebration of your body's capabilities and as a form of physical self-love.

<u>Self-Care Activities to Support Self-Love</u>

Create a Self-Care Kit:

Assemble a collection of items that bring you comfort and joy, such as your favorite book, a scented candle, soothing teas, or a cozy blanket. Turn to this kit whenever you need a reminder to care for yourself.

Nourishing Your Body:

Treat yourself to meals that not only nourish your body but also delight your senses. Cooking a favorite meal can be a meditative and loving act towards yourself.

Digital Detox:

Regularly schedule periods where you disconnect from digital devices and social media to reconnect with yourself. Use this time to engage in activities that you find restorative and enriching.

Self-Compassion Pause:

Implement a daily "self-compassion pause" where you check in with yourself, acknowledge how you're feeling, and offer yourself kindness and understanding, especially in challenging moments.

Nature Connection:

Spend time in nature to ground yourself and cultivate a sense of peace. Whether it's a walk in the park, tending to a garden, or simply sitting under a tree, connecting with nature can be a profound act of self-love.

Reflection and Action Steps

Embarking on the journey toward positive self-talk and embracing affirmations is a transformative process that requires intention, practice, and patience. Let's summarize some actionable steps to challenge negative self-talk and integrate affirmations into your daily life as well as offer some prompts for journaling and reflection to deepen your understanding and commitment to cultivating a nurturing internal dialogue.

Actionable Steps to Challenge Negative Self-Talk

Identify and Acknowledge: *Begin by recognizing moments of negative self-talk. When you catch yourself engaged in self-criticism, pause and acknowledge the presence of these thoughts without judgment.*

Question and Challenge: *Ask yourself whether these negative statements are truly accurate. Challenge them by considering evidence that contradicts these beliefs and by looking at the situation from a more balanced perspective.*

Shift Perspective: *Replace negative self-talk with positive affirmations or neutral, fact-based statements. Focus on your strengths, achievements, and the effort you're putting into your growth.*

Practice Mindfulness: *Cultivate a practice of mindfulness to help you stay present and avoid spiraling into negative thought patterns. Mindfulness can help you observe your thoughts without getting caught up in them.*

Seek Support: *Sometimes, challenging negative self-talk can be difficult to do alone. Don't hesitate to seek support from friends, family, or professionals who can help you navigate through this process.*

Integrating Affirmations into Daily Life

➤ Write affirmations that resonate with your personal values, goals, and the aspects of yourself you wish to affirm or develop. Ensure they are positive, in the present tense, and feel authentic to you.

Here are a few examples to get you started:

"I am worthy of love and respect just as I am."
- This affirmation encourages acceptance of oneself without conditions or changes, promoting a sense of intrinsic worth.

"I choose to treat myself with kindness and patience." - This statement emphasizes the choice to approach oneself with the same compassion and understanding that one would offer to a friend.

"My mistakes do not define me; they guide my growth." - This shifts the perspective on mistakes from being marks of failure to valuable lessons that contribute to personal development.

"I am enough, and my happiness comes from my own accomplishments and qualities." - This affirmation reinforces the idea that self-worth should be internally derived and not based on external validation or achievements.

"I embrace who I am and let go of who I think I'm supposed to be." - This encourages the acceptance of one's true self, letting go of societal or external expectations that may not align with one's authentic identity.

"Every day, in every way, I am becoming a better version of myself. - This positive statement promotes continuous self-improvement and the belief in one's ability to grow and change positively over time.

➤ Set specific times throughout your day for affirmation

practice—perhaps in the morning, during a break, or before going to bed. Consistency is key.

➤ Place affirmations where you will see them regularly—on your mirror, computer, or phone. Visual cues can serve as constant reminders of your commitment to positive self-talk

➤ Dedicate a few minutes each day to meditate with your affirmations. Repeat them silently or aloud, focusing on the feelings they evoke.

Journaling and Reflection Prompts

1. *What negative self-talk patterns have I noticed in myself? What triggers them?*

2. *How do these patterns affect my feelings and behaviors?*

3. *What evidence contradicts the negative beliefs I hold about myself?*

4. *Write down three personalized affirmations that counteract your common negative thoughts. How do these affermations make you feel?*

5. *Reflect on a situation where positive self-talk or affirmations changed your perspective or outcome. What did you learn from this experience?*

Step 1: Reflection

Begin with a few minutes of quiet reflection. Consider the aspects of yourself and your life that you appreciate, as well as areas where you seek growth or healing.

Write down three qualities you love about yourself and three areas you wish to improve upon or offer yourself more kindness.

Step 2: Crafting Your Affirmations

For each of the three qualities you love, write an

affirmation that reinforces that positive attribute.

* Example: *"I am [deeply compassionate with myself and others.]"*

For each of the areas you wish to improve or show kindness, craft an affirmation that supports growth and self-compassion as if the goal is already achieved.

* Example: *"I am [growing stronger and more resilient each day.]"*

Step 3: Visualization

Close your eyes and visualize yourself embodying the affirmations. Imagine feeling the emotions and experiencing the growth or healing they promote.

Step 4: Commitment

Choose one or two affirmations to focus on for the coming week. Plan a specific time each day to repeat them to yourself, such as in the morning, during a break, or before bed.

(Optional) Step 5: Share and Reflect

Consider sharing your affirmations with family and/or friends. Opening up about your intentions to those who care for and support you can enhance your journey towards authenticity, while also providing a nurturing environment for your aspirations to flourish.

Conclusion: Embracing the Language of Self-Love

Creating rituals around self-love and self-care activities reinforces our commitment to nurturing our relationship with ourselves. These practices serve as reminders of our worth and our commitment to personal growth. Affirmations serve as a tool to reinforce our values, goals, and self-worth. They are not just positive statements but declarations of our truth, helping to manifest a self-image that is aligned with our deepest desires for personal growth and fulfillment.

Through this chapter, you've experienced how internal dialogue shapes our reality, impacting our self-perception, emotions, and behaviors. By becoming aware of and actively shifting from negative to positive self-talk, we open ourselves to a world of self-acceptance and empowerment. This chapter has highlighted the importance of treating ourselves with the same kindness and understanding we would offer to a dear friend. Self-compassion is a critical component of self-love, allowing us to navigate life's challenges with grace and resilience. Let the principles and practices outlined in this chapter be your guide as you continue to explore the depths of your being. Remember, self-love is the foundation upon which a fulfilling life is built. By nurturing a loving and compassionate relationship with yourself, you set the stage for deeper connections with others and a life that truly reflects your innermost values and desires. Through understanding the impact of self-talk, recognizing and challenging negative narratives, and embracing the practice of affirmations and self-compassion, you have laid the groundwork for a relationship with yourself that is rooted in kindness, acceptance, and love.

As we move forward, let's remember that the language of self-love is not always spoken in grand gestures but often in the quiet moments of daily life. It's in the gentle reminders of our worth, the celebration of our achievements (no matter how small), and the compassionate embrace of our flaws and vulnerabilities. I encourage you to commit to practicing self-love and compassion as ongoing acts of gratitude towards yourself. This commitment is not a destination to be reached but a journey to be experienced, filled with growth, learning, and endless opportunities for discovery.

CHAPTER 3: EMBRACING VULNERABILITY

Vulnerability is the emotional risk, exposure, uncertainty, and courage it takes to be ourselves—in the face of both fear and joy. It's about showing up and being seen, even when there are no guarantees. The concept of vulnerability is often shrouded in myths and misconceptions, the most pervasive being its association with weakness. This misunderstanding can lead us to build walls around our true selves, preventing us from forming deep connections and living authentically. Yet, at its core, vulnerability is a profound strength, a gateway to genuine relationships, authenticity, and personal empowerment. Choosing to be vulnerable requires immense courage and strength. It means stepping into the arena, fully aware of the risk of judgment or rejection, yet choosing to remain open and authentic.

Vulnerability is not about revealing every detail of our lives to everyone we meet. It's about emotional honesty and the willingness to express our true thoughts, feelings, and desires where appropriate and with people who have earned the right to hear them. Many believe they can choose whether or not to be vulnerable. In reality, vulnerability is an inherent part of the human experience. Our choice lies not in avoiding vulnerability but in how we respond to it—whether we embrace it as a path to authenticity or shield ourselves to our detriment.

Embracing vulnerability allows us to form deeper, more genuine connections with others. By showing our true selves, we invite others to do the same, fostering relationships built on trust and authenticity. Living vulnerably means living authentically. It involves honoring our feelings, desires, and boundaries, and expressing them openly. This authenticity is liberating, allowing us to lead lives aligned with our true selves. Vulnerability is empowering. It teaches us that we can face fear, uncertainty, and emotional exposure and emerge stronger. Each act of vulnerability builds resilience, teaching us that we are capable of handling life's challenges.

Understanding the Fear of Vulnerability

Understanding and confronting the fears associated with vulnerability is not a task to be undertaken lightly. It requires courage, self-compassion, and patience. These fears, deeply rooted in our desire to protect ourselves from pain, can prevent us from experiencing the richness of genuine connections and living authentically. By identifying your fears, you begin to dismantle the barriers to vulnerability, paving the way for deeper connections with others and a more authentic relationship with yourself. Remember, vulnerability is not about weakness but about finding strength in the courage to be seen and known.

Exploring Common Fears and Barriers

Fear of Rejection: *Perhaps the most prevalent fear is that of being rejected. This fear stems from the concern that if we show our true selves, we will not be accepted or loved. It's a protective mechanism, guarding us against the pain of not belonging.*

Fear of Judgment: *Closely related to the fear of rejection is the fear of being judged. We worry that our weaknesses, mistakes, or simply the essence of who we are might be deemed insufficient or unworthy by others.*

Fear of Feeling Exposed: *To be vulnerable is to allow ourselves to be seen, truly and fully. This exposure can be terrifying, as it leaves us open to potential criticism and hurt. It challenges our need for control and the safety of our emotional armor.*

Activities to Identify Your Own Fears

Activity 1: Fear Mapping

Create a "fear map" related to vulnerability. On a piece of paper, write down situations where you find it difficult to be vulnerable. For each situation, identify the underlying fear (rejection, judgment, exposure). Recognizing these fears is the first step toward addressing them.

Activity 2: Journaling Prompts

Use journaling to explore your fears around vulnerability. Some prompts might include:

1. *"What does vulnerability mean to me?"*

2. *"What experiences have taught me that being vulnerable is unsafe?"*

3. *"How have I benefited from being vulnerable in the past?"*

4. *"What might change if I allowed myself to be more vulnerable?"*

Activity 3: The Worst-Case Scenario Exercise

Consider a situation where you're hesitant to be vulnerable. Write down the worst-case scenario, detailing what you fear might happen. Then, reflect on how you would cope with or address this scenario. Often, you'll find that you are more resilient and capable of handling potential outcomes than you initially thought.

Activity 4: Vulnerability Practice

Choose a safe and supportive setting to practice vulnerability. This could be sharing a personal story, expressing a hidden talent, or admitting a mistake. Start small and gradually increase your level of openness as you become more comfortable.

Vulnerability and Self-Discovery

Each moment of openness and honesty with ourselves and others is an opportunity to learn, grow, and move closer to our authentic selves. Through these exercises, you'll begin to see vulnerability not as a source of fear or weakness but as a powerful tool for self-discovery.

The Essential Role of Vulnerability in Self-Discovery

Vulnerability acts as a mirror, reflecting our most authentic selves back to us. It demands honesty and courage, asking us to acknowledge and accept our flaws, desires, and dreams. This process of opening up, though daunting, is incredibly rewarding. It peels away the layers we've constructed to protect ourselves, revealing the core of who we are. This revelation is crucial in understanding our true selves and determining the direction of our personal journey.

Reflective Exercises for Exploring Vulnerability

Exercise 1: Vulnerability Timeline

Create a timeline of significant moments in your life where you felt vulnerable. This could include times when you took a risk, faced a fear, or opened up about something personal.

* Next to each event, note how you felt before, during, and after. Reflect on what these moments taught you about yourself.

Exercise 2: The Lessons Learned Journal

Dedicate a section of your journal to explore the lessons learned from moments of vulnerability.

* For each instance, consider what you discovered about your strengths, weaknesses, values, and

capacity for resilience. How did these moments contribute to your understanding of yourself?

Exercise 3: The Vulnerability Dialogue

Engage in a reflective dialogue with yourself about a recent moment of vulnerability.

* Write this as a conversation in your journal, starting with expressing the vulnerability and then responding with kindness, understanding, and encouragement, as a friend might. - *This exercise helps to internalize a supportive approach to dealing with vulnerable moments.*

Exercise 4: Gratitude for Vulnerability

Reflect on and write about instances where being vulnerable led to positive outcomes, such as strengthened relationships, personal growth, or a newfound sense of freedom.

* Express gratitude for these moments and the courage it took to be vulnerable. Recognizing the value in these experiences reinforces the benefit of vulnerability in our lives.

Building Trust with Yourself

Before we can fully open up to others, we must first cultivate a sense of safety and security within ourselves. This self-trust is foundational; it assures us that we can handle the outcomes of our vulnerability, whether they are positive or negative. Developing self-trust involves nurturing an inner dialogue that supports and reassures us, especially during moments of vulnerability.

<u>Techniques for Developing Self-Trust</u>

1. Acknowledge Your Strengths and Achievements:

   Regularly take stock of your strengths, achievements, and the challenges you've overcome. This practice reinforces the belief in your capabilities and resilience, foundational aspects of self-trust.

2. Set and Achieve Small Goals:

   Build trust in yourself by setting small, achievable goals and following through on them. Each achievement, no matter how minor, strengthens your confidence in your ability to commit and succeed.

3. Practice Self-Compassion:

   Develop a compassionate inner voice that supports you, especially in times of failure or disappointment. Self-compassion is a key component of self-trust, as it assures you that you are worthy of kindness and understanding, irrespective of outcomes.

4. Reflect on Past Vulnerabilities:

   Reflect on times you've been vulnerable in the past and how you've navigated those experiences. This reflection can highlight your capacity to handle vulnerability and the growth that has come from those experiences, reinforcing trust in yourself.

<u>Tips for Cultivating a Supportive Inner Dialogue</u>

1. Speak to Yourself as You Would a Friend:

   In moments of vulnerability or self-doubt, address yourself as you would a dear friend. Offer words of encouragement, understanding, and reassurance.

2. Use Affirmations to Build Confidence:

   Employ affirmations that bolster your self-esteem and trust in your own judgment. Phrases like "I trust my intuition" or "I am capable of handling whatever comes my way" can be powerful reminders of your self-reliance.

3. Practice Mindfulness to Stay Present:

   Mindfulness practices can help you stay grounded in the present moment, reducing anxiety about the future or regret about the past. This presence can foster a more supportive and less critical inner dialogue.

4. Challenge Negative Thoughts:

   When you notice negative or self-doubting thoughts, challenge them. Ask yourself whether they are based on fact or fear, and consciously replace them with more supportive and trusting messages.

Creating Safe Spaces
for Vulnerability

Embracing vulnerability requires environments and relationships that support safe spaces and allow us to share our true selves without fear of judgment or rejection. Creating safe spaces for vulnerability is both an external and internal process. Externally, it involves cultivating relationships and environments that encourage openness and authenticity. Internally, it requires building a foundation of self-trust and self-compassion, allowing you to approach vulnerability with confidence and resilience.

Creating and Identifying Supportive Environments

1. Assessing Relationships for Safety:

   Evaluate your relationships to determine which ones feel safe for vulnerability. Look for qualities like empathy, non-judgment, and active listening. Trust your instincts about where you feel most valued and understood.

2. Cultivating a Culture of Openness:

   In your relationships and communities, actively encourage and model vulnerability. Share your thoughts and feelings openly when you feel safe, and respond to others' vulnerability with compassion and empathy.

3. Choosing the Right Moment:

   Timing can significantly impact the receptiveness of vulnerability. Choose moments for sharing that feel natural and where the other person is likely to be receptive and attentive.

Strategies for Setting Boundaries and Communicating Needs

1. Establishing Clear Boundaries:

   Boundaries are essential for creating safe spaces. Clearly communicate your limits regarding what you are willing to share and the type of feedback you find helpful. Boundaries help manage expectations and foster mutual respect.

2. Expressing Needs Directly:

Be upfront about your needs in vulnerable situations, whether you're seeking advice, empathy, or simply a listening ear. Clear communication prevents misunderstandings and ensures that your needs are met.

3. Practicing Active Listening:

Foster safe spaces by being an active listener. Show genuine interest, avoid interrupting, and reflect back what you've heard to show understanding. Active listening encourages reciprocal openness.

4. Nurturing Trust Gradually:

Trust is built over time. Start by sharing smaller vulnerabilities and gradually move to more significant ones as trust deepens. This gradual approach helps ensure the safety of the space for deeper sharing.

Creating a Personal Safe Space

1. Self-Soothing Techniques:

Develop personal strategies for self-soothing when facing vulnerability, such as mindfulness, deep breathing, or engaging in a comforting activity.

* These techniques can provide a sense of safety and grounding.

> **Mindful Breathing:** *Sit or lie down in a comfortable position. Close your eyes and take a slow deep breath through your nose, filling your lungs completely. Hold your breath for a moment, then exhale 3x as slowly through your mouth. As you breathe out, visualize releasing any tension or negativity, focusing solely on the rhythm of your breath.*

Progressive Muscle Relaxation (PMR): *Begin in a comfortable seated or lying position. Start with your feet and work your way up to your face. Tense each muscle group (e.g., calves, thighs, glutes, abdomen, arms, hands, and face) tightly, but without straining, for about five seconds, then relax it completely for 10 seconds. Notice the warmth and relaxation that follow the muscle tension. This method is especially effective for reducing physical tension and the physiological symptoms of stress.*

Guided Imagery: *Find a quiet place where you won't be interrupted. Close your eyes and imagine a place where you feel completely at ease. This could be a beach, a quiet forest, a favorite childhood spot, or anywhere that brings you peace. Visualize this place in as much detail as possible—the sights, sounds, and smells. Allow yourself to feel the tranquility of the scene as if you were there. Spend 5-10 minutes in this space, letting its serenity soothe your mind.*

2. Journaling:

Use journaling as a private space to explore your vulnerabilities. Writing can be a therapeutic way to process emotions and experiences in a safe, personal context.

Explore Self-Compassion: *Write a letter to yourself from the perspective of a compassionate friend. What would you say to someone with your struggles? How might you encourage the person to accept and love themselves fully?*

Set Boundaries for Healing: *What are some boundaries you need to establish to protect your emotional energy? Consider relationships, work, and personal habits. How can setting these boundaries be an act of self-love?*

Visualize Your Best Self: *Imagine a version of yourself who fully embraces their vulnerabilities and loves* *themselves unconditionally. What does a day in their life look like? What steps can you take to start embodying this version of yourself today?*

* *Sometimes, creating a safe space for vulnerability involves seeking support from a therapist or counselor. Professional guidance can offer a confidential and supportive environment for exploring and embracing vulnerability.*

The Role of Vulnerability in Relationships

By intentionally introducing and nurturing vulnerability in our interactions, we create a foundation of trust, understanding, and deep emotional connection. By showing our true selves, complete with our fears, hopes, and dreams, we can foster that level of understanding and closeness and how it can transform our relationships into sources of strength, support, and profound intimacy.

<u>Deepening Intimacy Through Vulnerability</u>

The Foundation of Trust:

Vulnerability helps to build trust, a fundamental element of any strong relationship. By opening up and showing our authentic selves, we invite others to do the same, creating a mutual trust that deepens over time.

Enhancing Emotional Connection:

Sharing vulnerabilities allows for a deeper emotional connection, as it signals to the other person that they are trusted and valued. This shared emotional landscape can strengthen the bond between individuals.

Fostering Empathy and Understanding:

Being vulnerable gives others insight into our experiences and emotions, fostering empathy and a deeper understanding of each other's worlds. This empathy is crucial for compassionate and supportive relationships.

<u>Introducing Vulnerability into Relationships</u>

Start Small:

Begin with small disclosures and gradually increase the depth of your sharing as your comfort level grows. This approach allows both parties to adjust to the increasing levels of openness at a comfortable pace.

Choose the Right Time and Place:

Select moments for vulnerability that are conducive to open, uninterrupted conversations. A quiet, private setting can create a safe space for sharing.

Use Conversation Starters:

Employ open-ended questions that encourage deep sharing, such as *"What's something you've always wanted to do and why?"* or *"Is there something you've never told anyone but wish you could?"*

* Here are a few more examples of conversation starters to help create a safe space and discuss vulnerabilities with someone you trust. These can also be used as journal prompts for self-reflection and discovery of your own vulnerabilities.

"What's one thing you wish more people understood about you that you rarely express?" - This prompt invites your partner to reveal deeper aspects of their personality and experiences that are not typically visible to others.

"When you're going through a tough time, how can I help you feel more supported and understood?" - This question not only shows your willingness to support them during vulnerable times but also opens up a conversation about their needs and how they handle difficulties.

"Do you feel like there are parts of your emotions or experiences that you keep protected? What do you think holds you back from sharing them?" - Discussing barriers to openness can help both of you understand each other's boundaries and hesitations, fostering empathy and support.

Engage in Shared Activities:

Participate in activities that naturally lend themselves to vulnerability, such as collaborative art projects, cooking together, or outdoor adventures. These shared experiences can create opportunities for open dialogue.

Practice Active Listening:

When someone is being vulnerable with you, practice active listening. Show that you value their openness by giving them your full attention, reflecting back what you've heard, and offering support without judgment.

Examples of this would be:

"It sounds like you're saying (....), Did I get that right?" - This encourages clarification and deeper exploration of the issue.

"What part of (....) feels most overwhelming?" - Such questions help to encourage deeper reflection and more awareness of feelings and possible underlying triggers vs the surface situation.

"What can I do to help?" - This shows that you are there to support them, not just to offer unsolicited advice.

Be Patient:

Remember that deepening intimacy through vulnerability is a process that takes time. Be patient with yourself and others as you navigate the complexities of building closer, more authentic relationships.

<u>Nurturing Vulnerability in Established Relationships</u>

Regular Check-ins:

In established relationships, regularly check in with each other about your feelings, dreams, and challenges. These check-ins can keep the lines of communication open and ensure that both parties feel heard and valued.

Express Gratitude:

Show appreciation for the other person's willingness to be vulnerable. Expressing gratitude can reinforce the positive aspects of openness and encourage continued sharing.

Seek Mutual Growth:

Use vulnerability as a tool for mutual growth, exploring ways you can support each other's aspirations and work through challenges together.

Embracing Vulnerability as a Path to Empowerment

Recognize that vulnerability is an integral part of being human and a powerful force for personal transformation. By committing to this practice, you open yourself up to a world of possibilities, where growth, empowerment, and authenticity await. Embrace vulnerability not as a one-time act but as a continuous practice essential to authentic living.

The Transformative Power of Vulnerability

Personal Growth Through Vulnerability:

Consider the idea of a person who, after years of hiding their true passions for fear of judgment, finally shares their art with the world. The act of making themselves vulnerable not only opens doors to new opportunities but also brings a profound sense of fulfillment and authenticity.

Vulnerability and Connection:

The possiblity that two people who, by sharing their deepest fears and insecurities, forge a bond that is both deeper and more resilient than they ever imagined possible. This vulnerability becomes the bridge to a connection that is rich with understanding and mutual support.

Vulnerability as a Catalyst for Change:

Think about an individual who, by openly discussing their struggles with mental health, inspires others to seek help and start their own journeys of healing. This vulnerability not only empowers the individual but also creates ripples of change that positively impact the community.

Embracing Vulnerability in Everyday Life

Vulnerability as Practice:

Embracing vulnerability means recognizing it as a daily practice. It's about choosing authenticity in small moments—whether it's admitting a mistake at work, expressing love to a family member, or asking for help when needed. Each act of vulnerability strengthens our courage and deepens our connections.

Creating Spaces for Vulnerability:

Actively seek and create spaces where vulnerability is welcomed and nurtured. This might mean initiating conversations about feelings and experiences, participating in support groups, or engaging in activities that encourage emotional expression, like art or writing.

Vulnerability and Self-Compassion:

As you practice vulnerability, remember to extend compassion to yourself. Not every act of openness will be met with the response you hope for, but every effort is a step towards a more authentic and empowered self.

Encouragement for the Journey Ahead

Remember, vulnerability is not a sign of weakness but a testament to your strength and courage. It's the path to discovering your true self, building meaningful relationships, and living a life that resonates with your deepest values and aspirations.

Reflection and Action Steps

As we conclude this exploration of vulnerability, let's reflect on the key takeaways and consider actionable steps and reflective exercises to incorporate vulnerability into our lives in safe and meaningful ways.

Summary of Key Takeaways

➤Vulnerability is Strength: It requires courage to show up authentically and share our true selves, making vulnerability a form of bravery, not weakness.

➤Foundation for Connections: Vulnerability deepens relationships, fostering intimacy and trust by allowing us to see and be seen genuinely.

➤Path to Authenticity: Living vulnerably aligns our external lives with our internal values and desires, leading to a more authentic and fulfilling existence.

➤Empowerment through Vulnerability: Each act of vulnerability strengthens our resilience, teaching us that we can face fear and uncertainty with grace.

Actionable Steps to Practice Vulnerability

Start Small: *Begin by sharing small vulnerabilities with trusted friends or family members. Notice how these moments of openness impact your relationships.*

Listen Actively: *Cultivate an environment of vulnerability by being an active and empathetic listener when others share with you.*

Self-Reflection: *Regularly engage in self-reflection to understand your fears and resistance to vulnerability. This understanding can guide your journey towards openness.*

Seek Feedback: *After being vulnerable, consider asking for feedback from the person you shared with. This can provide* *insights into how your vulnerability is perceived and the impact it has on your relationships.*

Journal Prompts and Reflection Questions

1. What does Vulnerablility mean to me? Why does it feel challenging

2. Recall a time when being vulnerable led to a positive outcome. What did I learn from that experiance?

3. What fears or beliefs hold me back from being more open and vulnerable?

4. How can I create a safe space for myself and others to share more openly?

5. What are three small steps I can take this week to practice vulnerability?

Conclusion: The Courage to Be Vulnerable

This journey through understanding fear, building self-trust, creating safe spaces, deepening relationships, and recognizing vulnerability as a source of empowerment underscores a fundamental truth: embracing vulnerability is not a sign of weakness but a courageous act of strength. By daring to be vulnerable, we open ourselves to the full spectrum of human experiences, allowing us to connect more deeply with others, embrace our true selves, and live lives rich with authenticity and meaning.

This journey has illuminated the role of vulnerability in:

> *Fostering Deep Connections: Vulnerability allows us to show our true selves, inviting others to do the same, and deepening our connections in the process.*

> *Building Self-Trust: Through vulnerability, we learn to trust ourselves, recognizing our resilience and our capacity to navigate the complexities of life.*

> *Creating Safe Spaces: Vulnerability encourages the creation of environments where openness and authenticity are valued and nurtured.*

> *Empowering Personal Growth: Embracing vulnerability propels us toward personal growth, teaching us valuable lessons about strength, courage, and the human spirit.*

Remember, vulnerability is not a one-time event but a continuous practice—an integral part of living authentically.

Part 2:
Building Authentic Connections

CHAPTER 4:
COMMUNICATION IS KEY

Whether in our personal lives, professional environments, or casual interactions, the way we exchange information, express our feelings, and articulate our needs profoundly impacts the strength and quality of our connections. Despite its importance, many find effective communication challenging, often falling into pitfalls that can lead to misunderstandings, frustration, and conflict.

<u>Some common communication pitfalls</u>

Assuming Rather Than Asking: Making assumptions about what others think or feel without direct inquiry can lead to misunderstandings.

Poor Listening Skills: Failing to listen actively, interrupting, or planning a response while the other person is still talking can prevent a true understanding of their message.

Avoiding Difficult Conversations: Evading discussions about sensitive topics can lead to unresolved issues and resentment.

Non-Verbal Miscommunication: Body language, tone of voice, and facial expressions can sometimes contradict verbal messages, leading to confusion.

Overuse of Digital Communication: Relying too heavily on text messages or emails for important conversations can result in misinterpretation of tone and intent.

<u>Key principles of effective communication</u>

Active Listening: Engage fully with the speaker, offering your undivided attention and reflecting back what you've heard to ensure understanding.

Clarity and Conciseness: Express your thoughts and feelings clearly and directly, avoiding ambiguity.

Empathy: Strive to understand the emotions behind the words, responding with sensitivity to the speaker's feelings.

Assertiveness: Communicate your needs and boundaries confidently and respectfully, without aggression or passivity.

Openness to Feedback: Be willing to receive and constructively respond to feedback, viewing it as an opportunity for growth.

Non-Verbal Awareness: Pay attention to and align your body language, facial expressions, and tone of voice with your verbal messages.

Understanding Communication Styles

Identifying and understanding our communication style is crucial for building healthy relationships, resolving conflicts, and conveying our thoughts and feelings clearly. The four primary communication styles—assertive, passive, aggressive, and passive-aggressive. Remember, communication styles can evolve with intention and practice, leading to healthier, more connected relationships.

<u>Exploring Communication Styles</u>

1. Assertive Communication:

Assertive communicators express their thoughts, feelings, and needs directly and respectfully. They stand up for their rights while considering the needs and rights of others. This style is characterized by clear, honest expression and active listening, fostering mutual respect and understanding.

Assertive communication builds trust and respect. It leads to open, honest relationships where both parties feel heard and valued.

2. Passive Communication:

Passive communicators often avoid expressing their thoughts and feelings to avoid conflict. They may comply with others' demands at the expense of their own needs and rights.

This style can lead to resentment and unmet needs. Passive communicators may feel overlooked or undervalued, while those around them may be unaware of their true feelings or desires.

3. Aggressive Communication:

Aggressive communicators express their needs and opinions in a way that violates the rights of others. This style is often characterized by loud, demanding speech, criticism, and dominance.

Aggressive communication can lead to fear, resentment, and a breakdown in trust, damaging relationships over time.

4. Passive-Aggressive Communication:

Passive-aggressive communicators express their negative feelings indirectly rather than addressing issues openly. This style may involve sarcasm, backhanded compliments, or subtle sabotage.

* *This style can create confusion, frustration, and mistrust among parties, as the communicator's true feelings and intentions are obscured.*

<u>Self-Assessment Exercises</u>

1. Reflect on Recent Interactions:

Think about a recent conversation that was significant to you. Write down how you expressed yourself, how you felt, and the outcome. Reflect on which communication style your behavior most closely resembles.

2. Identify Your Patterns:

Keep a journal for a week, noting instances where you communicated in ways that felt significant. At the end of the week, review your entries to identify patterns in your communication style.

3. Seek Feedback:

Ask close friends, family members, or colleagues for honest feedback about how they perceive your communication style. Compare this feedback with your self-assessment.

The Art of Listening

Active listening is more than a communication technique; it's a way of being present and engaged to fully understand the speaker's message. It's a skill that fosters empathy, deepens connections, and enhances interpersonal relationships. This practice not only enriches your interactions but also fosters a sense of community and understanding, creating deeper bonds with those around you.

Techniques for Improving Listening Skills

Maintain Eye Contact: *Eye contact is a non-verbal signal that shows you are engaged and focused on the speaker. It encourages trust and helps you stay attentive.*

Use Encouraging Body Language: *Nodding, leaning slightly forward, and keeping an open posture are signs of active engagement. These non-verbal cues can encourage the speaker to continue and open up more fully.*

Provide Feedback: *Reflect back what you've heard by paraphrasing or summarizing the main points. This not only shows you're actively listening but also clarifies any misunderstandings right away.*

Avoid Interrupting: *Allow the speaker to finish their thoughts without interruption. This shows respect for their perspective and gives you a complete understanding of their message.*

Ask Open-Ended Questions: *Encourage deeper insights and further conversation by asking questions that require more than a yes or no answer.*

Activities to Practice Empathy and Understanding

1. Reflective Listening Exercise:

Pair up with a partner and take turns sharing a personal

story or opinion. The listener should practice active listening techniques, then reflect back the main points or emotions they heard.

This exercise can enhance empathy and understanding by encouraging both parties to engage deeply with the other's perspective.

2. Daily Listening Intention:

Set a daily intention to practice one aspect of active listening in your conversations, whether it's maintaining eye contact, asking open-ended questions, or providing feedback.

* Reflect on your experiences and any changes in your interactions.

3. Empathy Journal:

Keep a journal where you note down conversations in which you practiced active listening, focusing on how it affected the depth of connection and understanding. Reflect on any challenges you faced and how you might overcome them in future conversations.

Expressing Needs and Desires

The ability to articulate our needs, desires, and boundaries clearly and confidently is a fundamental aspect of self-care and relationship maintenance. While it may feel daunting at first, developing this skill is essential for your emotional well-being and the health of your relationships.

<u>Guidance on Expressing Needs and Desires</u>

1. Self-Reflection:

   Begin with introspection to clearly understand what your needs and desires are. Reflect on what is non-negotiable for your well-being and what you wish for in your relationships and life. Being clear about these internally makes it easier to articulate them to others.

2. Use "I" Statements:

   Frame your needs and desires in the form of "I" statements to own your feelings and avoid placing blame. For example, "I feel valued when we spend quality time together," instead of "You never spend time with me."

3. Be Direct but Kind:

   Clarity does not equate to harshness. You can be direct about your needs and boundaries while still being kind and empathetic. Ensure your tone and choice of words reflect respect for both yourself and the listener.

4. Practice Active Listening:

   When expressing your needs, be prepared to listen to the other person's perspective. This reciprocal understanding can lead to more meaningful solutions that respect both parties' needs and desires.

Tips for Overcoming Fear and Discomfort

1. Start Small:

   If you're new to expressing your needs, start with smaller, less emotionally charged topics to build your confidence. Gradual practice will make it easier to address more significant issues.

2. Prepare and Rehearse:

   If you're apprehensive about a conversation, it can be helpful to prepare and even rehearse what you want to say. Writing down your thoughts or practicing in front of a mirror can clarify your message and boost your confidence.

3. Establish a Safe Environment:

   Choose a comfortable, private setting for sensitive discussions. Initiating conversation in a safe, calm environment can reduce anxiety for both parties.

4. Acknowledge and Validate Feelings:

   Recognize that it's normal to feel vulnerable when expressing needs and desires. Remind yourself that your feelings are valid, and expressing them is a step toward healthier relationships.

5. Seek Support if Needed:

   If you find it particularly challenging to express your needs, consider seeking support from a friend, family member, or professional. They can offer guidance, perspective, and encouragement.

Navigating Difficult Conversations

Difficult conversations are an inevitable part of life. Whether it's addressing a problem, expressing dissatisfaction, or discussing a sensitive topic, the way these conversations are approached can significantly influence their outcome. By employing the techniques in this section, you can approach these challenging discussions with confidence, aiming for outcomes that respect and meet the needs of all involved.

<u>Strategies for Approaching Difficult Conversations</u>

1. **Prepare and Plan:**

Before initiating a challenging discussion, take time to reflect on what you wish to convey. Identify your main points, desired outcome, and any potential reactions the other person might have.

- ➢ Outline for preparing a difficult conversation:
  - o Define the Purpose of the Conversation
    - Identify the main goal: What do you hope to achieve?
    - Ensure the purpose is constructive: Is it to clear up misunderstandings, share feelings, resolve a conflict?
  - o Understand Your Feelings and Perspectives
    - Reflect on your emotions surrounding the issue.
    - Consider why this conversation is important to you.
  - o Anticipate Their Perspective
    - Try to predict their feelings and reactions.
    - Reflect on their past behavior in similar situations to better prepare for their possible responses.

➢ Structure of the Conversation
  o Opening the Conversation
    ▪ Start with a positive affirmation or appreciation if possible.
    ▪ Clearly state the purpose of the discussion.
  o State Your Views and Feelings
    ▪ Use "I" statements to express your feelings and avoid blaming.
    ▪ Be concise and specific about what is bothering you.
  o Invite Their Perspective
    ▪ Encourage them to share their views and feelings.
    ▪ Show openness and willingness to listen by using prompts such as, "How do you feel about this situation?"
  o Discuss and Explore the Issue
    ▪ Identify points of agreement and disagreement.
    ▪ Ask open-ended questions to explore these areas further.
  o Problem Solving
    ▪ Brainstorm possible solutions together.
    ▪ Discuss the pros and cons of these solutions.

2. Choose the Right Time and Place:

Timing and setting are crucial. Choose a private and neutral location where both parties feel comfortable and ensure there are no time constraints that could rush the conversation.

➢ Manage your Emotions
  o Stay Calm and Composed
    ▪ Monitor your emotions: Take deep breaths or pause if you feel overwhelmed.
    ▪ Keep your voice calm and avoid raising it.
  o Listen Actively
    ▪ Show empathy through body language and verbal cues.

- - Validate their feelings, even if you disagree.
  - o Avoid Escalation
    - - Steer clear of accusations, generalizations, and ultimatums.
    - - Take a break if the conversation gets too heated.

- ➤ Closure and Reflection
  - o Summarize and Agree
    - - Recap what was discussed and any agreements made.
    - - Express gratitude for the other person's openness and willingness to discuss the issue.
  - o Assess the Outcome
    - - Reflect on what went well and what could have been better.
    - - Consider your feelings and whether you felt heard and understood.
    - - Reflect on how the conversation has affected your relationship.

Techniques for Handling Difficult Conversations

1. Stay Calm and Composed:

Maintaining your composure is key. Practice deep breathing or pause for a moment if you feel your emotions rising. Remaining calm helps keep the conversation productive and respectful.

2. Practice Active Listening:

Listen to understand, not to respond. Allow the other person to express their thoughts and feelings without interruption. Reflect back what you've heard to ensure you've understood them correctly.

3. Use "I" Statements to Express Your Perspective:

Frame your thoughts and feelings using "I" statements to avoid sounding accusatory. For example, "I feel upset when..." rather than "You always..."

4. Seek to Understand the Other Person's Perspective:

Empathize with the other person's viewpoint, even if you don't agree. Understanding their perspective can help you find common ground and work towards a mutually beneficial solution.

5. Focus on Solutions, Not Blame:

Shift the conversation towards finding a solution rather than dwelling on blame. Collaborate to identify steps both parties can take to resolve the issue and prevent similar problems in the future.

Techniques for Finding Mutually Beneficial Solutions

Brainstorm Together:

Encourage an open exchange of ideas for resolving the issue. Brainstorming together fosters cooperation and can lead to creative solutions.

Compromise When Necessary:

Be willing to compromise and find a middle ground. A solution that partially meets both parties' needs is often more sustainable than a winner-takes-all approach.

Agree on Follow-Up Actions:

Conclude the conversation with agreed-upon actions and steps. This ensures both parties are committed to moving forward and addresses the issue at hand.

The Importance of Non-Verbal Communication

Non-verbal communication plays a pivotal role in how our messages are received and interpreted. It encompasses body language, facial expressions, tone of voice, and other physical cues that, together, can complement, enhance, or even contradict our verbal messages. By becoming more aware of and skilled in using non-verbal cues, we can enhance our ability to communicate effectively, ensuring our intended message is clearly understood and appropriately received; as well as accurately interpret those of others.

<u>Understanding Non-Verbal Communication</u>

Body Language: Our posture, gestures, and movements convey a wealth of information about our confidence, openness, and attentiveness. For instance, crossed arms might be perceived as defensive, while leaning in slightly can signal interest and engagement.

Facial Expressions: The human face is incredibly expressive, capable of conveying complex emotions without a single word. Smiles, frowns, and eye movements can all add nuance to our verbal messages or offer clues to our true feelings.

Tone of Voice: The way we say something often carries more weight than the words themselves. Tone, pitch, and pace can express enthusiasm, sarcasm, anger, or comfort, influencing how our message is received.

<u>Exercises for Enhancing Non-Verbal Awareness</u>

Exercise 1: The Mirror Practice

Spend a few minutes each day talking in front of a mirror. Pay attention to your facial expressions, gestures, and posture. Notice how small changes in your non-verbal cues can alter the perceived meaning of your words.

Exercise 2: People-Watching with a Purpose

In a public place, observe people interacting. Without listening to their conversation, try to infer the nature of their relationship and the mood of their exchange based on their non-verbal cues.

* This exercise can sharpen your ability to read non-verbal signals.

Exercise 3: The Silent Conversation

Partner with a friend or family member for a "silent conversation" where you communicate solely through non-verbal means for a few minutes.

Afterwards, discuss what you were each trying to convey and how accurately you were able to understand each other.

Exercise 4: Tone of Voice Awareness

Record yourself reading a neutral text, then listen to the playback, focusing on your tone of voice.

Experiment with different tones to convey various emotions and note how the same words can carry different meanings depending on how they're said.

Exercise 5: Feedback Loop

Ask for feedback from trusted friends or colleagues about your non-verbal communication. Are there signals you're sending unintentionally?

* Use this feedback to become more conscious of your non-verbal expressions and adjust as needed.

Enhancing Emotional Intelligence in Communication

Emotional intelligence (EI) plays a critical role in effective communication, influencing how we perceive and express ourselves, navigate social complexities, and make personal decisions that achieve positive results. It's about being aware of our own emotional states and those of others, and adjusting our communication accordingly.

The Role of Emotional Intelligence in Communication

Recognizing Emotions: The first step in emotional intelligence is becoming aware of your own emotions and those of the people you are communicating with.

* *This awareness can inform how you approach conversations and respond to others.*

Understanding Emotions: Grasping the cause and effect of emotions allows for deeper insight into behavioral patterns and reactions.

* *Understanding why a person feels a certain way can lead to more empathetic and tailored communication.*

Managing Emotions: The ability to regulate your emotions, particularly in stressful or challenging situations, ensures that your communication remains effective and appropriate.

* *Managing emotions also involves helping others regulate their emotional responses, fostering a conducive environment for constructive dialogue.*

Using Emotions: Leveraging emotions to facilitate different communication tasks, such as problem-solving or decision-making, can enhance the quality of interactions.

Emotional information can guide thinking and behavior, enriching the communication process.

<u>Strategies for Developing Emotional Intelligence</u>

1. Practice Self-reflection:

Regularly reflect on your emotional responses to different situations. Consider what triggered your emotions and how they influenced your behavior.

Self-reflection enhances self-awareness, a key component of EI.

2. Enhance Your Emotional Vocabulary:

Expand your vocabulary for emotions to articulate your feelings more precisely.

* Being able to describe your emotions accurately can improve how you communicate your emotional state to others.

3. Develop Empathy through Active Listening:

Practice active listening to truly understand the emotional content of what others are saying. Pay attention not just to the words, but to the tone of voice, facial expressions, and body language.

Empathy strengthens your ability to connect with others on an emotional level.

4. Respond, Don't React:

Learn to pause and choose your response in emotional situations instead of reacting impulsively.

* This pause can help you consider the most constructive way to express your emotions and address the issue at hand.

5. Seek Feedback:

Ask for feedback from trusted individuals about your emotional responses and communication style.

* Feedback can provide valuable insights into how your emotions and communication affect those around you.

6. Practice Stress Management Techniques:

Effective stress management supports emotional regulation. Techniques such as deep breathing, mindfulness, and physical exercise can help keep your emotions in check, enhancing your communication under pressure.

** These exercises are designed to be quick, simple, and effective, making them perfect for incorporating into daily routines or for moments when stress feels overwhelming.*

1. Five Senses Exercise: *This grounding technique involves using all your senses to focus on the present moment, which can help derail spiraling thoughts. Spend a minute on each sense:*

Sight: Look around and name five things you can see. Note their colors and textures.

Touch: Acknowledge four objects you can touch around you. Describe their texture, temperature, and shape.

Sound: Close your eyes and list three sounds you hear. Try to find sounds you usually overlook.

Smell: Identify two smells, whether pleasant or unpleasant. If you can't immediately smell anything, walk to an area where you can.

Taste: Savor a piece of candy or a sip of a drink. Describe the flavors and sensations.

2. Progressive Muscle Relaxation: *This technique reduces stress and anxiety by tensing and then relaxing each muscle group:*

Start with your feet and work your way up to your face.
- Tense each muscle group for five seconds and then relax for 30 seconds.
- Pay attention to the sensation of release in each area of your body and breathe deeply as you shift from one group to the next.

3. **Guided Imagery:** *Visualize a serene environment to escape the stress of everyday life:*

- Sit comfortably or lie down in a quiet place.
- Close your eyes and imagine a peaceful place, whether a quiet beach, a breezy mountain top, or a cozy room.
- Focus on the details in your environment—the sounds, scents, and sensations.
- Spend 5-10 minutes in this place, enjoying the peace and tranquility. Breathe deeply and allow yourself to feel calm and refreshed.

Reflection and Action Steps

This chapter has explored various facets of effective communication, from understanding different styles and the art of listening to expressing needs and managing emotions intelligently. As we reflect on these insights, remember enhancing communication skills is a continuous journey and it's crucial to integrate what we've learned into our daily lives and relationships.

Key Takeaways

➢ Understanding Communication Styles: Recognizing your own style and adapting to others can improve interactions.

➢ The Art of Listening: Active listening fosters empathy and connection.

➢ Expressing Needs and Desires: Clear, direct communication of your needs and boundaries is essential for healthy relationships.

➢ Navigating Difficult Conversations: Approaching challenging discussions with preparation and empathy can lead to constructive outcomes.

➢ Non-Verbal Communication: Being aware of and aligning your body language with your words enhances your message.

➢ Emotional Intelligence: Recognizing and managing emotions in yourself and others is key to effective communication.

Practical Steps to Improve Communication

➢ Daily Active Listening Practice: Choose one conversation each day to practice active listening, focusing entirely on the other person without planning your response.

➤ Express a Need or Desire: Once a week, practice expressing a need, desire, or boundary clearly and respectfully to someone close to you.

➤ Reflect on Non-Verbal Cues: After social interactions, reflect on the non-verbal cues you observed in others and what you conveyed through your body language.

➤ Emotional Intelligence Reflection: End each day by noting an emotion you felt strongly and how it influenced your communication. Consider how you might manage similar emotions in the future.

➤ Seek Feedback: Regularly ask friends, family, or colleagues for feedback on your communication style and areas for improvement.

<u>Journal Prompts and Reflection Questions</u>

1. What communication style do I predominantly use, and how has it affected my relationships?

2. Recall a recent conversation where I practiced active listening. What impact did it have on the interaction?

3. Describe a situation where my non-verbal communication could have been misinterpreted. How can I improve?

4. Reflect on a difficult conversation I had. What strategies did I use, and how effective were they?

5 How do my emotions influence my communication? Provide an example and explore alternative responses.

Conclusion: Committing to Open, Honest Communication

As we conclude our exploration of effective communication, it's important to reflect on the transformative power these skills hold in fostering authentic connections. Throughout this chapter, we've delved into the nuances of communication styles, the critical role of active listening, the importance of expressing our needs and desires clearly, navigating difficult conversations with grace, understanding the impact of non-verbal cues, and enhancing emotional intelligence to enrich our interactions. Each of these elements contributes to a comprehensive approach to communication that, when practiced, can significantly deepen our relationships and improve our understanding of ourselves and others.

The key to enriching your interpersonal interactions lies in understanding and adapting communication styles, mastering the art of listening, expressing your needs and desires clearly, navigating difficult conversations with tact, and using non-verbal cues effectively. Emotional intelligence also plays a crucial role in all forms of communication. By actively applying these principles and techniques, you're not just enhancing your ability to communicate effectively, you're also opening the door to deeper, more meaningful relationships. Embrace this journey with an open heart and a willing mind. Keep striving for improvement, not perfection, and watch as every conversation becomes a bridge to greater understanding and collaboration.

As you move forward, I encourage you to apply these insights with intention and compassion—both for yourself and for those you communicate cwith. The path to effective communication is paved with patience, practice, and a willingness to learn from each interaction. By embracing open, honest communication, you empower yourself to build stronger relationships, resolve conflicts constructively, and express your true self with confidence.

CHAPTER 5: LISTENING WITH EMPATHY

Meaningful communication transcends the act of hearing words, to fully engaging with, and understand, the speaker's emotions, thoughts, and perspective. It is an active process that requires not just attention to what is being said, but also a deep sensitivity to the emotions behind the words. In both personal and professional contexts, empathetic listening can bridge divides, heal conflicts, and deepen connections, making it an invaluable skill in fostering relationships built on trust and mutual understanding.

While active listening involves giving full attention to the speaker and providing feedback, empathetic listening goes a step further by delving into the emotional content of what is being shared. Empathetic listening encompasses active listening but adds a layer of emotional resonance and connection.

In personal relationships, empathetic listening strengthens bonds by demonstrating care, respect, and validation. It allows individuals to feel seen and understood, which is fundamental to emotional intimacy and trust. In professional settings, it fosters collaboration and trust among team members, enhances leadership effectiveness, and improves conflict resolution, as individuals feel more inclined to share openly and work together towards solutions when they feel genuinely heard.

The Basics of Empathy

Empathy encourages us to look beyond our own experiences and connect with others in meaningful, transformative ways. It involves more than simply recognizing another person's emotions; it's about genuinely understanding and feeling what another person is experiencing from within their frame of reference.

Defining Empathy

Empathy is the ability to perceive and relate to the thoughts, emotions, or experience of others, without having those feelings communicated explicitly.

The Three main components:

1. **Cognitive Empathy:** The intellectual understanding of another person's perspective or mental state.

2. **Emotional Empathy:** The capacity to physically feel the emotions of another as if they were contagious.

3. **Compassionate Empathy:** The combination of cognitive and emotional empathy to take action or show concern for another's well-being.

The Importance of Empathy in Human Connections

Empathy lies at the heart of all human relationships, serving as a bridge that facilitates genuine understanding and connection.

Building Trust: Empathy fosters trust, creating a safe space where individuals feel seen, heard, and valued.

Enhancing Communication: By understanding the emotions behind words, empathy enriches communication, making it more meaningful and effective.

Resolving Conflicts: Empathy allows for a deeper understanding of differing perspectives, facilitating conflict resolution and fostering mutual respect.

Strengthening Bonds: Empathetic connections deepen emotional bonds, leading to stronger, more resilient relationships.

Differentiating Between Sympathy and Empathy

While empathy and sympathy are often used interchangeably, they represent distinct concepts:

Sympathy involves acknowledging another person's emotional hardships and providing comfort and assurance. It's a feeling of care and concern for someone, often accompanied by a desire to see them happier or relieved of their distress.

Empathy, on the other hand, goes beyond simply recognizing or sharing in another's emotions. It involves a deeper engagement and understanding, putting oneself in another's shoes, and experiencing their feelings as one's own.

** This distinction is vital because empathetic listening brings a depth and authenticity to interactions that sympathy alone cannot.*

Barriers to Empathic Listening

Empathetic listening is a profound tool for deepening connections and fostering understanding. However, various barriers can impede our ability to listen empathetically. Recognizing and addressing these barriers is essential for cultivating a more present, open stance in our interactions.

<u>Common Barriers to Empathic Listening</u>

Distractions:

Both external (e.g., noise, technology) and internal distractions (e.g., wandering thoughts, preoccupation with personal issues) can detract from our ability to fully engage with the speaker.

Preconceptions and Judgments:

Entering a conversation with preconceived notions about the speaker or their situation can cloud our ability to listen without bias, limiting our empathetic response.

Emotional Reactions:

Strong emotional reactions to what is being shared can hinder empathetic listening. These reactions may stem from personal triggers or discomfort with the emotions being expressed.

The Fix-it Mentality:

The urge to offer solutions or advice rather than simply listening can prevent us from fully understanding and empathizing with the speaker's experience.

Lack of Patience:

Impatience for the speaker to get to the point or

to finish can lead to superficial listening, where the deeper emotional content of the message is missed.

Strategies for Overcoming Barriers

1. Minimize Distractions:

Create a conducive environment for listening by minimizing external distractions and making a conscious effort to set aside internal distractions.

2. Suspend Judgment:

Approach conversations with an open mind, consciously setting aside any preconceptions or judgments. Remind yourself that the goal is to understand the speaker's perspective and feelings.

3. Manage Emotional Reactions:

Recognize and acknowledge your emotional reactions without letting them dominate the conversation. Practice self-regulation techniques such as deep breathing to maintain your composure and presence.

4. Embrace Silence and Reflection:

Resist the urge to fill silence or immediately respond with advice. Use pauses to reflect on what is being shared and to formulate an empathetic response.

5. Cultivate Patience:

Develop patience by reminding yourself of the value of truly understanding and connecting with the speaker. Recognize that deep listening may require time and silence.

Skills for Empathetic Listening

Empathetic listening is a nuanced skill that goes beyond merely hearing words; it involves fully engaging with and understanding the speaker's emotions, intentions, and perspective. It requires a combination of active listening, non-judgmental acceptance, and emotional attunement.

<u>Developing Key Skills for Empathetic Listening</u>

* Active Listening:

Active listening is the foundation of empathetic listening. It involves giving your full attention to the speaker, using verbal and non-verbal cues to show engagement, and providing feedback that shows you have accurately received their message.

- Maintain eye contact, nod to show understanding, and use phrases like "I see" or "Go on" to encourage the speaker.

- Paraphrase or summarize what they've said to ensure clarity and understanding.

* Non-Judgmental Acceptance:

Approaching conversations with an open mind and withholding judgment allows the speaker to feel safe and supported. Non-judgmental acceptance is critical for fostering an environment where deep, meaningful communication can occur.

- Remind yourself that your role is to understand, not to evaluate

- Practice mindfulness to be aware of any biases or judgments that arise, consciously setting them aside.

* Emotional Attunement:

Emotional attunement involves tuning into the speaker's emotions and responding in a way that conveys understanding and empathy. It requires being sensitive to the emotional subtext of what is being communicated.

- Pay attention to non-verbal cues such as tone of voice, facial expressions, and body language to gauge the speaker's emotions.

- Reflect emotional content in your responses, such as saying, "It sounds like you're feeling frustrated," to validate their feelings.

Exercises to Practice Empathetic Listening Skills

Exercise 1: The Listening Mirror

Partner with a friend or family member and ask them to share something meaningful with you. Practice active listening and non-judgmental acceptance, then mirror back the content and emotions of their message.

** This exercise helps reinforce your understanding and shows the speaker they are truly heard.*

Exercise 2: Emotional Vocabulary Expansion

Each day, identify one emotion you feel and find three new words that describe nuances of this emotion.

** Expanding your emotional vocabulary enhances your ability to connect with and accurately reflect the emotions of others.*

Exercise 3: The Empathy Swap

Share a personal story with someone, then have them share one with you. Focus on emotionally attuning to their story and respond with empathy. Discuss afterwards how it felt to be on both sides of the empathetic listening process.

Exercise 4: Judgment Awareness Journal

Keep a journal for a week where you note any judgments that arise during conversations. Reflect on what triggered these judgments and how they might have impacted your ability to listen empathetically.

Use this awareness to practice setting aside judgments in future interactions.

Communicating Empathy

Empathy, when genuinely felt, is a powerful connector in human relationships. This involves more than just the right words; it encompasses verbal affirmations, reflective statements, and body language that together convey a deep sense of understanding and care.

Conveying Empathy Through Verbal Affirmations

Verbal affirmations are positive statements that recognize and validate another person's experience or feelings.

To communicate empathy

Use phrases that affirm the other person's feelings, such as "It sounds like you're really passionate about this," or "I can see why that situation would be upsetting."

Avoid phrases that dismiss or diminish the other person's feelings, even unintentionally, such as "It could be worse," or "You shouldn't feel that way."

Use Reflective Statements for Empathy

** Reflective statements involve paraphrasing or summarizing what the other person has said to show that you are actively listening and understand their perspective. This can be particularly effective in communicating empathy because it demonstrates that you are engaged and value what they are sharing.*

- Practice phrases like, "So, what I'm hearing is...," or "It seems like you feel...," to reflect back the speaker's thoughts or feelings accurately.

Body Language and Non-Verbal Cues

Non-verbal communication plays a significant role in expressing empathy. Your body language can reinforce the sincerity of your verbal messages or, if not congruent, can create confusion about your genuine feelings.

1. Maintain eye contact, lean in slightly, and nod to show you are engaged.

2. Be mindful of your facial expressions; they should match the emotion you are trying to convey.

3. Use open body language to show receptiveness, avoiding crossed arms or legs, which can appear defensive or closed off.

The Importance of Authenticity in Expressing Empathy

Authenticity is key when communicating empathy. Insincerity can be easily detected and can erode trust, making it harder for the other person to open up in the future.

To ensure your empathetic communication is authentic:

Connect with your own feelings of empathy before attempting to express them.
 * If you're struggling to find empathy for the other person's situation, ask more questions to better understand their perspective.

Be mindful of your tone of voice and choice of words. They should reflect genuine concern and interest.

Acknowledge if you're unsure of what to say.
 * Sometimes, admitting, *"I'm not sure what to say, but I'm really glad you told me,"* can be more empathetic than offering the perfect response.

The Role of Empathy in Conflict Resolution

Empathetic listening emerges as a powerful tool in conflict resolution; it's about leveraging these moments as opportunities for growth, understanding, and strengthening relationships. This approach not only resolves the immediate issue but also builds a foundation of trust and empathy that can prevent future misunderstandings and foster a more harmonious relationship ensuring that all parties' feelings and needs are acknowledged and respected.

Transforming Conflicts with Empathetic Listening

Empathetic listening in conflict situations involves more than just understanding the other person's point of view. It's about deeply connecting with their feelings and needs beneath the surface of the conflict.

** This approach can shift the dynamic from adversarial to cooperative, opening up new possibilities for resolution that satisfy everyone involved.*

Seeing Beyond the Argument: Empathy helps us see beyond the immediate issue to the underlying emotions and needs. Recognizing these deeper layers can shift the focus from winning the argument to finding a mutually beneficial solution.

Reducing Defensiveness: When parties in a conflict feel genuinely heard and understood, their defensiveness decreases. This openness fosters a more conducive environment for problem-solving and collaboration.

Techniques for Using Empathy in Conflict Resolution

Pause and Reflect: Before responding in a conflict, take a moment to consider the other person's perspective and feelings. This pause can prevent reactive responses and help you approach the situation with empathy.

Express Understanding: Use empathetic statements to convey that you understand the other person's point of view and feelings, even if you don't agree with them. Phrases like, "I see why you feel that way," or "It makes sense to me that you're upset about this," can validate their experience.

Ask Open-Ended Questions: Encourage dialogue and deeper understanding by asking questions that invite the other person to share more about their feelings and needs. Questions like, "Can you tell me more about what's bothering you?" or "What do you need from me to resolve this?" can open up the conversation.

Seek Common Ground: Use empathy to identify shared feelings, needs, or goals. Highlighting these commonalities can serve as a foundation for building solutions that consider everyone's well-being.

Offer Genuine Apologies: If appropriate, empathetic listening may reveal your role in the conflict. Offering a sincere apology that acknowledges the other person's feelings can be a powerful step toward resolution.

Collaborate on Solutions: Work together to find resolutions that address everyone's core needs and concerns. Empathetic listening can help uncover creative solutions that might not have been considered otherwise.

Empathy in Diverse Relationships

By consciously adapting empathetic listening techniques, you can deepen connections, resolve conflicts more effectively, and build a foundation of mutual understanding and respect across all areas of your life. Its application, however, needs to be nuanced to fit the unique dynamics of romantic partnerships, friendships, family interactions, and professional settings.

Empathy in Romantic Partnerships

In romantic relationships, empathy fosters intimacy and trust, allowing partners to feel deeply connected and supported. Empathetic listening in this context involves:

Validating Feelings: Acknowledge and validate each other's emotions without judgment. This reinforcement can strengthen emotional bonds and foster a safe space for vulnerability.

Navigating Conflicts: Use empathy to understand each other's perspectives during disagreements, focusing on finding solutions that address both partners' needs.

Empathy in Friendships

Friendships thrive on mutual understanding and respect, both of which are cultivated through empathy. To enhance empathy in friendships:

Be Present: Give your full attention when friends share their experiences, showing genuine interest and concern.

Share Experiences: Empathetically sharing your own experiences can create a two-way street of openness and trust.

Empathy in Family Dynamics

Family relationships, often complex, can benefit significantly from empathetic communication, which helps navigate the diverse personalities, roles, and expectations within a family. Implement empathy into family Dynamics by:

Acknowledging Individual Perspectives: Recognize and respect the individuality of family members, understanding that each person may have different emotional reactions and needs.

Facilitating Open Dialogue: Encourage family members to express their feelings and needs openly, fostering an environment of mutual support.

Empathy in Professional Settings

In the workplace, empathy can improve collaboration, leadership, and overall workplace culture. To apply empathy effectively in professional settings:

Promote Inclusivity: Show empathy by being attentive to diverse viewpoints and experiences, promoting an inclusive and supportive work environment.

Support Growth: Use empathetic listening to understand the aspirations and challenges of colleagues, offering support and encouragement for their growth and development.

Adapting Empathetic Listening Techniques

While the core principles of empathetic listening—such as validation, non-judgmental acceptance, and emotional attunement—remain constant, their application may vary based on the relationship type and individual needs. Consider the following when adapting empathetic listening:

Context Matters:

Adjust your approach based on the relationship's context and the situation at hand. Professional empathy, for example, might be more structured than in a casual friendship.

Individual Needs:

Pay attention to the unique emotional needs and communication preferences of those you're interacting with. Some may appreciate direct expressions of empathy, while others might find subtler gestures more meaningful.

Cultural Sensitivities:

Be mindful of cultural differences in expressing and receiving empathy. What constitutes empathetic communication can vary widely across cultures.

Reflection and Action Steps

This journey requires intention, practice, and a commitment to continuous self-improvement. Below are actionable steps and reflective prompts designed to help you cultivate your empathetic listening skills and encourage a self-assessment of your empathic abilities and areas for growth.

<u>Actionable Steps to Cultivate Empathetic Listening Skills</u>

- ➤ Practice Active Listening Daily:

  Choose at least one conversation per day to practice active listening. Focus entirely on the speaker, resist the urge to interrupt, and provide feedback that shows you are engaged.

- ➤ Engage in Reflective Listening:

  After the speaker has finished, summarize what you've heard and ask for clarification to ensure understanding. This not only validates the speaker but also deepens your comprehension of their perspective.

- ➤ Observe Non-Verbal Cues:

  Pay attention to body language, facial expressions, and tone of voice in your daily interactions. Reflect on how these non-verbal cues enhance your understanding of the speaker's emotions and intentions.

- ➤ Expand Your Emotional Vocabulary:

  Work on identifying and naming emotions more precisely, both in yourself and in others. This can enhance your ability to connect emotionally and communicate understanding more effectively.

- ➤ Seek Diverse Perspectives:

  Actively seek out conversations with people who have different backgrounds, experiences, and viewpoints. This can challenge and expand your empathetic understanding.

Journal Prompts and Reflection Questions

1. Reflect on Your Listening Habits:

   - In what ways do I find it challenging to listen empathetically?

   - What situations or emotions make active and reflective listening difficult for me?

2. Assess Your Emotional Attunement:

   - How accurately can I identify and understand the emotions of others?

   - Are there certain emotions I find harder to empathize with?

     - Why might that be?

3. Consider Your Non-Verbal Communication:

   - What non-verbal signals do I typically use when listening to others?

   - How might my body language affect the openness and trust in a conversation?

4. Evaluate Your Growth:

   - What progress have I made in my empathetic listening skills?

   - What situations have I noticed an improvement in my understanding and connection with others?

5. Identify Areas for Improvement:

   - What specific aspects of empathetic listening do I need to develop further?

   - How can I intentionally work on these areas in my daily interactions?

Conclusion: Living with Empathy

It's clear that this profound skill extends far beyond simple communication techniques, empathy, at its core, is a way of being—a lens through which we can view our interactions, relationships, and even ourselves. Living with empathy is a commitment to fostering a world where everyone feels seen, heard, and valued. By practicing empathy, we cultivate a more compassionate, inclusive, and supportive environment for everyone we encounter.

The Transformative Impact of Empathetic Listening

➤ Personal Growth: Empathetic listening challenges us to grow by stepping outside of our comfort zones and confronting our biases and preconceptions. It encourages self-reflection and fosters emotional intelligence, both of which are crucial for personal development.

➤ Relationship Enhancement: Empathy strengthens bonds by building trust and fostering open communication. It allows relationships to flourish based on mutual understanding, respect, and genuine connection.

➤ Conflict Resolution: By approaching disagreements with empathy, we can transform conflicts into opportunities for growth, finding solutions that honor all parties' needs and perspectives.

To live with empathy is to commit to understanding and connecting with others in a meaningful way. Here are some encouragements to integrate empathetic listening into your daily life:

➤ Practice Mindfulness: Stay present in your interactions, giving your full attention to the person you're engaging with. Mindfulness enhances your ability to listen empathetically.

➤ Seek to Understand: Approach every conversation with the intention to understand, rather than to respond or judge. Let curiosity guide your interactions.

➤ Reflect on Your Experiences: Regularly take time to reflect on your conversations and relationships. Consider how empathy influenced the interaction and what you learned from it.

➤ Embrace Vulnerability: Allow yourself to be open and vulnerable, both in expressing your own emotions and in receiving those of others. Vulnerability is a powerful pathway to empathy.

➤ Expand Your Perspectives: Actively seek out and listen to stories and experiences that differ from your own. This practice can deepen your empathy and broaden your understanding of the diverse world we share.

CHAPTER 6: THE ROLE OF GRATITUDE IN RELATIONSHIPS

Gratitude, at its essence, is an acknowledgment of the value and goodness in our lives, often stemming from an appreciation of others' contributions to our well-being. It involves a reciprocal exchange of respect and value, reinforcing the positive dynamics within a relationship but it extends beyond mere politeness or a social nicety and acts as a relational glue that fosters deep appreciation, mutual respect, and enduring bonds. Grounded in psychological research, the benefits of gratitude are profound, significantly enhancing relational satisfaction and resilience. When gratitude is expressed, it not only affirms the efforts and kindness of others but also deepens our connection to them, creating a cycle of goodwill and appreciation.

Studies consistently show that expressions of gratitude between partners are strongly correlated with higher levels of relationship satisfaction. Gratitude helps individuals feel more positively towards their partner, perceive more positive behavior from them, and feel more comfortable expressing concerns about their relationship. Gratitude also fosters emotional resilience, enabling relationships to withstand challenges and conflicts more effectively. It acts as a buffer against negative emotions and stress, helping individuals maintain a positive outlook even in difficult times.

Regular expressions of gratitude contribute to the deepening of bonds between individuals. It builds a foundation of trust and mutual respect, essential components for lasting relationships. Gratitude also encourages prosocial behavior —not only in the giver and receiver but also among those who witness acts of gratitude. This creates a ripple effect that enhances the social fabric of communities, promoting a culture of kindness and generosity. Gratitude cultivates a positive environment that nurtures growth, happiness, and satisfaction. By acknowledging the contributions and value of others, gratitude shifts the focus from what is lacking to what is abundantly present.

Understanding Gratitude

Gratitude goes beyond mere acknowledgment of a kind deed or a favorable circumstance; it encompasses a deeper recognition and appreciation of the inherent value in others and the positive aspects of our connections. By distinguishing gratitude from indebtedness, we can ensure that our expressions of thanks enrich our relationships in healthy and meaningful ways.

Defining Gratitude in Relationships

Gratitude, when fostered within relationships, is a multifaceted emotion that involves:

Acknowledging Goodness:

Recognizing the goodness in our lives, often brought forth by the actions, presence, or support of others. It's about seeing the value and positivity that others contribute to our existence.

Appreciation of Value:

Beyond mere recognition, gratitude involves a heartfelt appreciation for the people in our lives, valuing their unique qualities, efforts, and the joy they bring.

Reciprocal Connection:

Gratitude strengthens the bonds between individuals by fostering a cycle of generosity and appreciation. It's an emotional exchange that enriches both the giver and the receiver.

Gratitude vs. Indebtedness

While gratitude and indebtedness may arise from the same act of kindness, they differ significantly in their impact on relationships:

Gratitude is a positive emotion that enhances our connection to others. It fills us with warmth and a desire to express our appreciation freely, without the expectation of anything in return. Gratitude is uplifting and strengthens relational ties by focusing on the value and joy shared between individuals.

Indebtedness, on the other hand, is a feeling of obligation to repay someone for their kindness. While not inherently negative, indebtedness can introduce a transactional element into relationships, where actions are motivated by the desire to settle a debt rather than genuine affection or appreciation. This can create an imbalance, potentially leading to stress and resentment.

<u>Healthy Expressions of Appreciation</u>

To cultivate healthy expressions of gratitude in relationships:

Be Specific:

> When expressing gratitude, be specific about what you're thankful for.
>
> * This specificity shows that you truly notice and value the contributions of others.

Sincerity is Key:

> Ensure that expressions of gratitude are sincere.
>
> * Authentic gratitude is felt more deeply and has a more significant impact on strengthening relationships.

Regular Practice:

> Integrate gratitude into your daily interactions.
>
> * Regular expressions of gratitude can transform the dynamic of your relationships, making them more positive and resilient.

Focus on the Giver:

> Highlight the qualities of the person you're thankful for, rather than solely focusing on how their actions benefited you.
>
> * This shifts the emphasis to their inherent value and

your appreciation of them as an individual.

Cultivating a Gratitude Mindset

Cultivating a 'Gratitude Mindset' requires intentional practice and reflection, but it can reshape our perspective, enabling us to focus on the positive aspects of our relationships, even during challenging times. By focusing on the positive contributions and value of others, we not only enhance our relationships but also contribute to a more appreciative and compassionate community. Gratitude, when practiced regularly, becomes more than just a mindset; it transforms into a way of life that brings joy, resilience, and deepened connections.

<u>Strategies for Developing a Gratitude Mindset</u>

1. Daily Gratitude Reflection:

   Begin or end each day by reflecting on three aspects of your relationships for which you are grateful. This could be a kind gesture, a supportive conversation, or simply the joy someone brings into your life. Regular reflection reinforces a habit of looking for the positive in others.

2. Gratitude Journaling:

   Maintain a gratitude journal dedicated to acknowledging the goodness in your relationships. Writing down your thoughts can deepen your appreciation and provide a tangible reminder of the positive connections in your life.

3. Express Gratitude Regularly:

   Make it a practice to express your gratitude to others often. Whether through a simple "thank you," a note, or a more significant gesture, regular expressions of gratitude strengthen bonds and encourage a reciprocal appreciation.

4. Mindfulness and Gratitude:

Incorporate mindfulness practices that focus on gratitude. Mindful meditation on gratitude can help center your thoughts on the present moment and the abundance of positive aspects in your relationships.

Exercises for Recognizing and Reflecting on the Contributions of Others

1. The Gratitude Visit:

Think of someone who has made a significant positive impact on your life, to whom you have never fully expressed your gratitude. Write a detailed letter to them, explaining the effect they've had on you.

   * Consider delivering and reading the letter to them in person.

2. Gratitude Mapping:

Create a "gratitude map" where you visually chart out your relationships and the positive aspects or moments associated with each.

   * This can help you see the interconnected web of support and kindness surrounding you.

3. Weekly Gratitude Sharing:

Set aside time each week to share gratitude with a friend, family member, or partner. Discuss what you are each grateful for in your relationship and in your lives more broadly.

   * This practice can open up new avenues of connection and appreciation.

4. Acknowledgment Rituals:

Establish rituals or traditions centered around expressing gratitude within your family or circle of friends. This could be as simple as sharing what you're thankful for during meals or creating a gratitude board where everyone can post notes of appreciation.

Expressing Gratitude Effectively

Authentic and thoughtful expressions of gratitude can have a profound impact on relationships, creating moments of joy and recognition that resonate deeply. By expressing gratitude, you not only bring joy to those you appreciate but also contribute to a cycle of kindness and positivity that uplifts everyone involved.

Guidelines for Authentic Gratitude

Be Specific:

When expressing gratitude, specificity can greatly enhance its significance. Rather than general statements of thanks, pinpoint exactly what you are grateful for and why. This specificity shows that you are truly attentive and appreciative of the other person's actions or qualities.

Choose the Right Medium:

Expressing gratitude doesn't always require spoken words; often, non-verbal gestures can convey your appreciation just as powerfully and can offer a tangible reminder of your appreciation that the recipient can revisit.

Personalize Your Gratitude:

Tailor your expressions of gratitude to the recipient's preferences and your relationship with them. Personalization shows that you have put thought into your gratitude and value your unique connection.

The Importance of Timing and Sincerity

Timing:

The impact of gratitude can be amplified by timely expression. Acknowledging a kind act or support soon after it occurs reinforces the value of the gesture. However, it's also never too late to express gratitude for something meaningful, even if time has passed.

Sincerity:

The sincerity of your gratitude is perhaps its most crucial aspect. Gratitude should come from a genuine place of appreciation and not be used as a means to an end. The authenticity of your expression can be felt and is what truly deepens connections.

<u>Expressing Gratitude in Various Forms</u>

Verbal Appreciation:

Don't underestimate the power of saying "thank you" with warmth and eye contact* if in person. Verbalizing your appreciation in person or through a phone call can convey your emotions effectively.

- For Acts of Kindness:
    - *"I really appreciate you doing [specific task]. It helped me more than you know."*
    - *"Thank you for going out of your way for me. I am truly grateful for your generosity."*

- At Work:
    - *"I want to express my thanks for your hard work on this project. Your dedication really made a difference."*
    - *"Thank you for your exceptional effort. Your attention to detail is really apperciated"*

- In Personal Relationships:
    - *"I'm so grateful to have you in my life. You bring me such joy and comfort."*
    - *"Thank you for being there for me. Having your support means the world to me."*

- General Appreciation:

- *"I just wanted to express how much I value you. Thank you for being you and in my life."*

Written Notes:

A handwritten thank-you note can offer a personal touch that stands out in today's digital age. It allows you to articulate your gratitude thoughtfully and provides a keepsake for the recipient.

Thank You Notes:

A handwritten thank you card expressing your appreciation for somone's kindness, support, or generosity can be a cherished gesture.

Appreciation Letters:

A more formal letter to acknowledge someone's significant impact on your life or career. This can be especially meaningful in professional settings or for more significant personal favors.

Post-It Notes:

Leave surprise notes in places like a colleague's desk or a family member's laptop, offering a quick and cheerful thank you for daily small favors.

Acts of Kindness:

Showing your gratitude through actions—such as returning a favor, offering support, or giving a thoughtful gift—can speak volumes. Acts of kindness demonstrate your gratitude in a tangible way.

Creative Expressions:

Consider creative ways to express your gratitude, such as making something by hand, sharing a meaningful book, or dedicating a social media post to the person you're thankful for. These unique expressions can make the moment of gratitude even more memorable.

Gratitude Through Gifts

- Personalized Gifts: Give a gift that relates to the person's interests or needs, showing that you pay attention to what matters to them.

- Gift Cards: A universally appreciated gesture, especially if you know the person's favorite stores or restaurants.

- Homemade Gifts: Bake cookies, make a craft, or create something unique that shows your appreciation through personal effort.

Public Acknowledgments

- Acknowledging in Meetings: Publicly thanking someone in a meeting can make them feel valued and appreciated in front of peers.

- Social Media Shoutouts: A public thank you post, tagging the person and briefly describing how they helped you, can be a modern way to show gratitude.

Gratitude in Everyday Interactions

Incorporating gratitude into daily interactions doesn't require grand gestures; often, it's the small, consistent acts of appreciation that carry the most weight. By consciously choosing to express gratitude, we not only enhance our relationships but also contribute to a more positive and supportive environment.

<u>Tips for Incorporating Gratitude</u>

1. Start Your Day with Gratitude:

   Begin each day by expressing something you're grateful for about someone you live with or work closely with.

   * This positive start can set the tone for the day and encourage a culture of appreciation in your immediate environment.

2. Acknowledge the Little Things:

   Don't wait for grand gestures to express gratitude. Acknowledge the small, everyday actions that make your life easier or more pleasant.

3. Use Technology to Your Advantage:

   Leverage technology to send quick notes of thanks or appreciation. A brief, thoughtful text or email can brighten someone's day and show that you're thinking of them, even amidst a busy schedule.

4. Make Gratitude a Family or Team Ritual:

   Incorporate gratitude into family dinners or team meetings by having each person share something they're grateful for.

   * This practice builds a collective sense of appreciation.

<u>Examples of Everyday Gratitude</u>

For Partners:

- Leave a note expressing appreciation for something specific they did recently, like tackling a household chore or supporting you during a stressful time.

- Verbally thank them for being part of your life, highlighting qualities you admire in them.

For Family Members:

- Acknowledge their efforts, big or small, in maintaining the home or contributing to the family's well-being.

- Show interest in their activities and express gratitude for the shared moments and experiences.

For Friends:

- Recognize the ways they enrich your life, whether through laughter, advice, or companionship, and make it a point to tell them.

- Celebrate their achievements and express your gratitude for having them in your life.

For Colleagues:

- Thank someone for their assistance on a project or for making a challenging task more manageable.

- Express appreciation for their positive attitude or work ethic, noting how it contributes to a better work environment.

Overcoming Barriers to Gratitude

While the benefits of gratitude in enhancing our relationships and overall well-being are well documented, many of us still find it challenging to consistently practice gratitude. Various barriers, from pride and a fear of vulnerability to simply taking others for granted, can hinder our ability to express gratitude. Additionally, expressing gratitude toward difficult situations or challenging individuals in our lives can seem particularly daunting. However, these challenging circumstances often provide the most profound opportunities for personal growth and deepening our practice of gratitude.

<u>Identifying Common Barriers to Gratitude</u>

Pride:

Pride can often stand in the way of expressing gratitude, as acknowledging others' contributions might feel like admitting a dependency or inability to achieve something on one's own.

Fear of Vulnerability:

Expressing gratitude requires a level of openness and vulnerability that can be daunting for many. There's a fear that such expressions may be perceived as weakness or may not be reciprocated.

Finding Value in Challenges:

Difficult situations, while uncomfortable and often painful, can teach us valuable lessons about resilience, determination, and personal strength.

Seeing Beyond the Surface:

Challenging people often trigger our growth in unexpected ways. By expressing gratitude for these individuals, we acknowledge their role in our personal development journey.

Taking Others for Granted:

In the hustle of daily life, it's easy to take the contributions of those around us for granted, especially those closest to us. Familiarity can sometimes dull our sense of appreciation.

<u>Strategies for Overcoming These Obstacles</u>

Cultivate Humility:

Recognize that acknowledging the help and kindness of others is a strength, not a weakness. Humility allows us to appreciate the roles others play in our successes and happiness.

Embrace Vulnerability:

Understand that vulnerability is a bridge to deeper connections. Expressing gratitude opens up a space for genuine interaction, fostering stronger bonds.

Transform Relationships:

Sometimes, expressing gratitude can defuse tension and transform relationships. Consider sharing your appreciation for something specific that a challenging person does well, or acknowledge their positive traits. This can sometimes encourage more positive interactions moving forward.

Practice Mindfulness and Meditation:

Incorporate mindfulness practices that focus on gratitude. Meditation sessions that encourage gratitude for life's broad spectrum, including its challenges, can shift your mindset to one more consistently centered on gratitude.

Reflect on how dealing with a challenging person or situation has strengthened your patience, empathy, or communication skills, and the personal growth you experienced as a result.

Set Regular Reminders:

Incorporate gratitude practices into your daily routine. Setting reminders to reflect on what you're grateful for or to express gratitude to someone can help make it a habit.

The Ripple Effect
of Gratitude

When gratitude is expressed, it doesn't just benefit the giver and the receiver; it sets off a chain reaction of positivity. The recipient of gratitude is more likely to feel valued and, in turn, express gratitude to others. This phenomenon, often referred to as the "ripple effect" of gratitude, underscores how expressions of thankfulness can initiate positive feedback loops

Gratitude's Influence on Social Circles and Community Well-being

In Relationships:

Gratitude acts as a catalyst for mutual appreciation and respect in personal relationships, deepening emotional connections and resilience against challenges.

In Workplaces:

A culture of gratitude in the workplace can lead to increased satisfaction, reduced stress, and higher productivity. Employees who feel appreciated are more motivated and likely to pass on their positive feelings through acts of kindness and recognition towards their colleagues.

In Communities:

When communities engage in acts of gratitude, whether through volunteerism, public acknowledgments, or support networks, a stronger sense of community emerges. Gratitude can bridge divides, encourage altruism, and create an environment where people feel connected and supported.

Reflection and Action Steps

By actively practicing gratitude, we can enhance the quality of our relationships, promote personal growth, and foster a greater sense of happiness and satisfaction in our lives. As you continue to integrate gratitude into your daily life, remember that the journey is ongoing. Each step taken towards recognizing and expressing gratitude is a step towards a more fulfilled and connected existence.

<u>Practical Steps to Foster Gratitude in Relationships</u>

➤ Daily Gratitude Lists:

Start or end each day by listing three things you are grateful for in your relationships. This could be specific qualities of a person, kind actions taken by someone, or moments of connection you experienced.

➤ Gratitude Letters:

Write letters of gratitude to people in your life for whom you are thankful. Describe in detail what they did and how it impacted you. Consider delivering these letters in person if possible.

➤ Gratitude Reminders:

Set daily reminders to pause and reflect on moments of gratitude throughout your day. This can help integrate gratitude into your routine.

➤ Gratitude Conversations:

Incorporate discussions of gratitude into your regular conversations with friends, family, or partners. Share what you're grateful for about each other and why.

➤ Acts of Kindness:

Show your gratitude through actions. Perform random acts of kindness for loved ones or even strangers as a way of expressing your appreciation for the positive aspects of your life and relationships.

<u>Journal Prompts and Reflection Questions</u>

1. What was I most grateful for today and why?

2. How did expressing gratitude (or receiving expresions of gratitude) make me feel?

3. In what ways have my relationships improved or changed as I've focused more on gratitude?

4. What barriers do I encounter when trying to express gratitude, and how can I overcome them?

5. How does practicing gratitude impact my overall outlook on life and my interactions with others?

6. Reflect on a situation where gratitude played a key role in resolving a misunderstanding or conflict. What did you learn from that experience?

7. When was the last time I expressed gratitude to someone, and how did it make me feel?

Conclusion: Gratitude as a Way of Life

It's clear that this profound practice offers far more than momentary expressions of thanks. Through the acknowledgment of the goodness in our lives, often brought forth by the contributions of others, it enriches our connections, enhances our emotional well-being, and fosters a greater sense of fulfillment. Let gratitude be your compass, leading you to a more connected, fulfilled, and heartfelt existence.

Key Insights and Benefits of Gratitude

> ➢ Deepening Connections: Regular expressions of gratitude can significantly deepen our relationships, making our bonds stronger and more resilient.

> ➢ Enhancing Emotional Well-being: Gratitude has the power to elevate our mood, reduce stress, and foster a general sense of happiness and contentment.

> ➢ Promoting Reciprocity: Gratitude encourages a cycle of kindness, where acts of appreciation lead to further gestures of kindness, creating a positive feedback loop within our social networks.

> ➢ Fostering Resilience: By focusing on what we have rather than what we lack, gratitude helps us navigate life's challenges with grace and resilience.

Integrating gratitude into our relational practices requires mindfulness and intentionality. It's about making a conscious choice to recognize and appreciate the value in others and the beauty in our relationships. Living gratitude involves taking time each day to reflect on whom and what we're grateful for. It's finding creative and meaningful ways to express our gratitude to others, whether through words, actions, or gestures. It's shifting our mindset to focus on gratitude in all aspects of life, making the effort to be fully present in our interactions, allowing us to appreciate the richness of our relationships and the moment.

Part 3:
Transforming Challenges into Opportunities

CHAPTER 7: NAVIGATING LIFE'S UPS AND DOWNS

Life's challenges can range from minor daily annoyances to significant life events that alter our course. These moments of difficulty, though often unwelcome, are not aberrations but are all part of the human experience. Acknowledging the inevitability of these challenges is the first step towards engaging with them constructively. This acceptance empowers us to shift our focus from avoidance to engagement, from mere survival to growth.

Resilience is the capacity to recover quickly from difficulties; it's a dynamic process that involves psychological, emotional, and behavioral flexibility and adaptation to stress and adversity. More than just a return to a pre-challenge state, resilience encompasses the ability to use challenges as springboards for personal development and positive change. It involves a complex interplay of factors, including our attitudes, coping strategies, and support systems.

Adopting a positive perspective in the face of challenges is a critical component of resilience. This approach doesn't imply a denial of hardship or a Pollyannaish optimism but rather a constructive engagement with reality. A positive perspective helps us to identify and leverage opportunities for learning and growth inherent in every challenge. It encourages a focus on strengths and possibilities rather than limitations and problems, significantly altering our experience of and response to adversity.

The transformative potential of challenges, when approached with resilience and a positive perspective, is immense. Difficulties can serve as catalysts for personal growth, self-discovery, and the deepening of our relationships. They can teach us about our strengths and weaknesses, clarify our values, and hone our problem-solving skills. This process of growth and development, fueled by the challenges we face, is a testament to the human spirit's adaptability and strength.

Recognizing Challenges
as Opportunities

The perspective we adopt in the face of life's challenges can significantly influence our experience and outcome. By shifting the narrative from one of victimhood to empowerment, it enables us to move through adversity with grace, learning valuable lessons, and building strength along the way.

Shifting the Narrative

Empowerment Through Perspective: The first step in transforming challenges into opportunities is altering our perspective. Instead of viewing challenges as insurmountable obstacles, we can see them as chances to develop new skills, gain wisdom, and emerge stronger. This shift from a victim mindset to one of empowerment and agency is crucial in changing how we experience and respond to adversity.

Learning and Growth: Every challenge carries with it the seeds of learning and growth. By approaching difficulties with curiosity and openness, we can uncover insights about ourselves and the world around us that enrich our understanding and personal development.

Exercises for Reframing Difficulties

1. Challenge Reflection Exercise:

Write down a recent challenge you faced. Next to it, list the skills you used or developed in response to this challenge, any personal strengths you discovered, and the lessons you learned. Reflecting in this way can help you see the positive aspects and growth opportunities that emerged from the difficulty.

2. The Opportunity Journal:

Keep an "Opportunity Journal" where you record daily or weekly challenges and the potential opportunities they present. Focus on how each challenge can contribute to your growth, resilience, or understanding. Over time, this journal can become a powerful reminder of your ability to find value in adversity.

3. Reframing Exercise:

Choose a challenge you're currently facing and write down your initial thoughts and feelings about it. Then, consciously try to reframe it by asking yourself: "What can I learn from this? How can this situation make me stronger? What positive outcomes might emerge?" Write down your answers, focusing on the potential for growth and empowerment.

4. Visualization Technique:

Visualize a challenging situation you've overcome in the past. Recall the feelings of accomplishment and strength that followed. Now, apply that same sense of resilience and capability to a current challenge, visualizing a positive outcome where you emerge empowered and enriched by the experience.

The Role of Gratitude
in Facing Challenges

Gratitude shifts our focus from what is lacking, to the abundance present in our lives. This shift in perspective can mitigate stress, and help to gain a more positive outlook that empowers us to navigate adversity with grace and strength. This perspective does not diminish the reality of our struggles but allows us to approach them with resilience and hope. By acknowledging the good, even in small doses, we buffer ourselves against the negative psychological impact of challenges.

Cultivating Gratitude in Difficult Times
Cultivating gratitude when times are tough may seem counterintuitive, but it is particularly during these periods that such a practice can be most beneficial.

Practical tips for fostering gratitude amidst adversity

1. Daily Gratitude Reflections:

   Dedicate a few moments each day to reflect on three things you are grateful for. These do not have to be grandiose; even simple joys or comforts can be profound. The consistent practice of identifying elements of gratitude in your daily life can shift your focus from adversity to abundance.

2. Gratitude Journaling:

   Keeping a gratitude journal can enhance your awareness of life's blessings. Regularly writing down what you are thankful for consolidates positive thoughts and feelings, making gratitude a more automatic response to life's challenges.

3. Mindfulness and Gratitude Practices:

   Incorporate gratitude into your mindfulness practice.

This can be as simple as paying attention to the present moment and acknowledging the aspects of your environment or experiences for which you are grateful. Mindfulness heightens our awareness of the present, allowing us to find gratitude in the here and now.

4. Gratitude Letters or Messages:

Writing letters or messages expressing gratitude to others can reinforce your sense of connectedness and support, vital components for navigating tough times. Expressing gratitude to others not only uplifts them but also reinforces your own feelings of gratitude and well-being.

5. Seek Gratitude in Challenges:

Actively look for something to be grateful for in the midst of a challenge. This might involve finding a lesson learned, recognizing your own strength or resilience, or appreciating the support of others during difficult times.

Building Emotional Resilience

Emotional resilience is the ability to navigate through life's adversities with strength and grace, learning and growing from challenges rather than being overwhelmed by them. By embracing vulnerability, practicing self-compassion, seeking support, and utilizing your inherent strengths, you can develop the resilience needed to navigate life's challenges effectively. Developing this ability is a dynamic process, one that involves a deep understanding of oneself and the proactive cultivation of inner resources.

<u>Strategies for Developing Emotional Resilience</u>

Embracing Vulnerability:

Recognize that vulnerability is not a sign of weakness but a courageous step toward growth. Embracing vulnerability allows us to face our fears, seek help when needed, and connect deeply with others, fostering resilience.

Practicing Self-Compassion:

Treat yourself with kindness and understanding, especially during difficult times. Self-compassion involves acknowledging your suffering, recognizing its common humanity, and being mindful of negative emotions without over-identifying with them.

Seeking Support:

Cultivate a supportive network of friends, family, or professionals who can provide encouragement and perspective. Seeking support is a strength, not a weakness, and is essential for building resilience.

Maintaining Physical Well-being:

Physical health significantly impacts emotional

resilience. Regular exercise, adequate sleep, and healthy eating habits can enhance your ability to cope with stress and bounce back from adversity.

Activities to Identify Sources of Strength

1. Make a list of your personal strengths and achievements. Reflect on how these qualities have helped you overcome past challenges.

   * Recognizing your strengths can boost your confidence and resilience in facing future adversities.

2. Think of a time when you faced a significant challenge and came through it stronger. Write about the experience, focusing on the strategies you used to cope and what you learned about your capacity for resilience.

3. Create a visual map of your support network, including friends, family members, colleagues, and professionals. Highlight the types of support each person provides and consider how you can engage with this network more effectively during times of need.

4. Keep a daily journal focusing on resilience-building activities. Each day, note any challenges you faced, how you responded, what strengths you utilized, and moments of gratitude or connection.

   * This practice can enhance your awareness of resilience in action.

5. Engage in mindfulness exercises or meditation to cultivate presence and awareness.

   * Mindfulness can help you manage stress, recognize and regulate emotions, and approach challenges with a clear, calm mind.

The Power of Perspective

Viewing challenges as opportunities for growth rather than insurmountable obstacles can fundamentally reframe our approach to problem-solving. This doesn't negate the reality of adversity, but allows us to engage with it more constructively and helps to cultivate resilience, fostering a sense of empowerment and possibility. By intentionally practicing perspective-shifting techniques and activities, we can cultivate a mindset that views adversity as a catalyst for growth.

<u>Finding Meaning in Difficulty:</u>
Looking for meaning in our struggles can provide a sense of purpose and direction. Understanding how challenges contribute to personal growth or how they can lead to new opportunities encourages a more optimistic engagement with adversity.

<u>Techniques for Maintaining a Positive Outlook</u>

Cognitive Restructuring:

This technique involves identifying and challenging negative thought patterns that contribute to feelings of despair or defeat. By questioning the validity of these thoughts and replacing them with more balanced and constructive ones, we can shift our perspective towards optimism and solution-finding.

Focusing on What Can Be Controlled:

Concentrating on aspects of a challenge that are within our control, rather than fixating on those that aren't, can significantly reduce feelings of helplessness and stress. This focus empowers us to take actionable steps towards resolution.

Practicing Gratitude:

Regularly acknowledging what we are grateful for, even

in the midst of difficulties, can shift our focus from what we lack to what we possess. This practice enhances our overall outlook on life, providing a buffer against negativity.

Seeking Out Positive Stories:

Reading or listening to stories of individuals who have overcome similar challenges can provide perspective, inspiration, and practical strategies for facing our own difficulties.

Visualization Techniques:

Visualizing positive outcomes can be a powerful motivator. Imagine overcoming the current challenge and reflect on the feelings of achievement and relief that come with resolution. This technique can provide the hope and strength needed to persevere.

Activities to Foster a Positive Perspective

1. Perspective-Shifting Exercise:

Write down a current challenge from your perspective, detailing your thoughts and feelings. Then, try to write about the same challenge from the viewpoint of someone you admire for their optimism and resilience.

* Notice the differences in perspective and what you can learn from this exercise.

2. Daily Positivity Log:

Keep a daily log of positive experiences, interactions, or accomplishments. Reviewing this log during challenging times can remind you of the positive aspects of your life and help maintain an optimistic outlook.

3. Solution-Focused Brainstorming:

Set aside time to brainstorm potential solutions or positive outcomes to a current challenge. Encourage creativity and open-mindedness, focusing on the wide range of possibilities rather than immediate limitations.

Staying Grounded
in the Present

It's easy to become overwhelmed by what lies ahead or fixated on what has passed. Staying grounded in the present moment offers a powerful antidote to the stress and anxiety that accompany adversity. Mindfulness and presence not only help manage these feelings but also enhance our clarity, decision-making, and overall well-being. By focusing on the present, we can reduce anxiety and stress, making space for more constructive responses to adversity.

Managing Stress and Anxiety:

Stay Present

Staying present allows us to observe our thoughts and emotions without judgment, providing the clarity needed to make informed decisions. This clear-headedness is crucial when navigating complex situations or making tough choices.

Reducing Overwhelm:

Engaging in mindfulness can help diminish feelings of overwhelm by anchoring us in the here and now. This focus on the present moment prevents us from becoming consumed by potential future problems or past regrets.

Guided Practices for Staying Grounded

1. Focused Breathing Exercise:

Begin by finding a comfortable and quiet space. Close your eyes and take a deep breath in through your nose, filling your lungs completely. Hold your breath for a moment, then exhale slowly through your mouth. Concentrate on the sensation of the air moving in and out of your body. Repeat this process for several minutes, returning your focus to your breath whenever your mind wanders.

2. Sensory Grounding Technique:

This practice involves tuning into your immediate sensory experiences to anchor yourself in the present. Notice five things you can see, four things you can touch, three things you can hear, two things you can smell, and one thing you can taste. Engaging your senses in this way can quickly bring your focus back to the present moment.

3. Mindful Observation:

Choose an object from your immediate environment and focus all your attention on it. Observe it as if you're seeing it for the first time, noting its color, shape, texture, and any other qualities. This exercise in mindful observation can help redirect your focus from worries and stress to the simplicity of the present moment.

4. Mindful Walking:

Take a short walk, focusing entirely on the experience of walking. Pay attention to the movement of your body, the sensation of your feet touching the ground, and the sounds around you. Mindful walking combines physical activity with mindfulness, providing a dual benefit of stress reduction and gentle exercise.

5. Gratitude Moments:

Take a few minutes each day to reflect on aspects of your current situation or environment for which you are grateful. This practice of gratitude can shift your focus from what's wrong to what's right, fostering a sense of contentment and presence.

Leveraging Support Networks

During challenging times, the value of support networks becomes unmistakably clear. These networks, composed of family, friends, colleagues, and even broader community resources, provide a vital lifeline, offering emotional support, practical assistance, and a sense of belonging. Equally important is our role within these networks, not just as recipients of support but as active contributors to the well-being of others. A culture of mutual care ensures that all members feel valued and supported, fostering a strong, resilient community.

The Importance of Support Networks

Emotional and Practical Support:

Support networks can offer both emotional solace and practical help, from a listening ear to direct assistance with daily tasks. This dual support can significantly alleviate the stress and isolation that often accompany challenges.

Sense of Belonging:

Being part of a support network reinforces a sense of belonging and community, reminding us that we are not alone in our struggles. This connection is essential for maintaining hope and resilience.

Asking for Help

Be Specific in Your Requests:

When seeking support, clarity is key. Be specific about what you need, whether it's someone to talk to, help with errands, or professional advice. Clear requests make it easier for others to provide the assistance you need.

Overcome Reluctance:

Many people hesitate to ask for help due to fear of burdening others or appearing vulnerable. Remember that seeking support is a sign of strength, not weakness. Most people are more than willing to help if they understand your needs.

Utilize Various Channels:

Don't limit yourself to one avenue of support. Reach out across your network, including friends, family, professional services, and community groups. Diversifying your sources of support can provide a broader range of perspectives and assistance.

Offering Support to Others

Listen Actively:

Sometimes, the best support you can offer is a willing, attentive ear. Listen actively, without rushing to offer advice, to truly understand what the other person is experiencing.

Offer Practical Assistance:

Actions often speak louder than words. Offering practical help, such as running errands, preparing meals, or assisting with tasks, can be incredibly supportive.

Check-In Regularly:

Regular check-ins can make a world of difference. A simple message or call to let someone know you're thinking of them can provide comfort and reassurance during tough times.

Cultivating a Community of Mutual Care

Foster an Environment of Openness:

Encourage an atmosphere where seeking and offering help is normalized and celebrated. Sharing your own experiences of giving and receiving support can inspire others to do the same.

Build and Maintain Connections:

Invest time and effort into building and maintaining your support network. Regular social interactions, even if they're not focused on support, can strengthen bonds and ensure a foundation of trust and familiarity.

Reflection and Action Steps

By actively engaging with these strategies and reflecting on your experiences, you can continue to cultivate the skills and mindsets necessary to transform life's challenges into valuable opportunities for growth. Remember, the journey through adversity is not just about enduring but about thriving, learning, and emerging stronger on the other side.

Actionable Strategies Recap

➤ Recognize Challenges as Opportunities: Shift your mindset to view challenges as chances for growth, learning, and development.

➤ Cultivate Gratitude: Practice gratitude regularly, even during tough times, to maintain a positive outlook and appreciate the good in your life.

➤ Build Emotional Resilience: Embrace vulnerability, practice self-compassion, and seek support when needed to strengthen your emotional resilience.

➤ Maintain a Positive Perspective: Use cognitive restructuring to maintain optimism and focus on what you can control during challenging times.

➤ Stay Grounded in the Present: Incorporate mindfulness practices to stay present and reduce overwhelm, enhancing clarity and decision-making.

➤ Leverage Support Networks: Draw on and contribute to your support networks for emotional and practical assistance during difficult periods.

Journal Prompts and Reflection Questions

1. Reflect on a recent challenge and identify at least one opportunity for growth it presented. How did this challenge contribute to your personal development?

2. Write about three things you are grateful for this week, focusing on why they are meaningful to you. How does practicing gratitude change your perspective on daily life?

3. Think about a time when you demonstrated resilience in the face of adversity. What strategies did you use, and how can you apply them to future challenges?

4. Describe a situation where changing your perspective helped you overcome a challenge. What did you learn from this experience about the power of perspective?

5. Recall a moment when being fully present helped you navigate a difficult situation. What mindfulness techniques did you use, and how did they impact the outcome?

6. Reflect on the role of support networks in your life. How have you both contributed to and benefited from these networks during challenging times?

Conclusion: Embracing Life's Journey

This chapter has illuminated strategies for recognizing challenges as opportunities, leveraging gratitude, building emotional resilience, maintaining a positive perspective, staying grounded in the present, and drawing strength from our support networks. Each of these elements contributes to a holistic approach to life's ups and downs, empowering us to face the future with confidence, resilience, and an open heart.

By embracing challenges as catalysts for personal development, we can transform our experiences of adversity into sources of strength and wisdom. The practice of gratitude opens our eyes to the abundance that surrounds us, even in the midst of difficulty, fostering a sense of contentment and well-being.

The strategies discussed in this chapter are tools that build emotional resilience and equip us to bounce back from setbacks, while maintaining a positive perspective. Staying grounded in the present moment ensures that we do not become overwhelmed by what lies ahead or burdened by what has passed. In embracing life's journey with all its complexities, we discover a sense of grace and gratitude.

An open heart is essential as we move forward and through life's inevitable ups and downs. Embracing life's journey with connections, based on mutual care and understanding, provides a safety net that catches us when we fall and lifts us higher than we could ever reach alone.

CHAPTER 8: FROM CONFLICT TO CONNECTION

Conflict, often viewed with apprehension and regarded as a harbinger of discord, is, in reality, an inescapable and natural aspect of human relationships. Far from being merely a source of division, conflict holds within it the seeds of growth, understanding, and relational deepening—if approached with a constructive and mindful attitude.

While avoiding conflict might seem like the path of least resistance, it often leads to resentment and distance. Contrary to the belief that conflict is inherently destructive, approaching disagreements with respect, openness, and a willingness to understand can transform them into constructive experiences that contribute to the relationship's resilience and depth. The key lies not in avoiding conflict but in how it is managed.

Conflict challenges us to examine our beliefs, behaviors, and the dynamics of our relationships and this introspection can lead to personal growth and a deeper understanding of both ourselves and others. Navigating conflict constructively opens channels of communication that encourages a shift from avoidance to engagement. It provides a platform for expressing needs and vulnerabilities, fostering empathy and a richer understanding of each other's experiences and viewpoints.

Successfully working through differences and finding common ground reinforces trust and commitment, proving that the relationship can withstand challenges and provides a space for mutual growth.

Understanding the Sources of Conflict

Conflict in relationships often stems from a variety of sources. From unmet needs and differing values to communication breakdowns, understanding the root causes of disagreements is the first step toward constructive resolution.

Common Sources of Conflict

Unmet Needs:

One of the most prevalent sources of conflict arises from unmet needs, whether emotional, physical, or psychological. When individuals feel that their essential needs are not being acknowledged or satisfied within a relationship, frustration and conflict can emerge.

Differing Values:

Differences in values, beliefs, and priorities can lead to conflict, especially when parties feel that their core values are being compromised or disrespected. These differences often reflect deeper aspects of identity and worldview, making conflicts based on values particularly challenging to navigate.

Communication Breakdowns:

Many conflicts are not about substantive issues but rather result from misunderstandings, misinterpretations, and ineffective communication. Breakdowns in communication can escalate minor disagreements into major disputes, obscuring the real issues at hand.

Exercises for Identifying Underlying Issues

1. Needs Assessment Exercise:

Write down a recent conflict you've experienced and ask yourself, "What needs of mine were unmet in this situation?" Consider all dimensions of your needs —emotional, physical, and psychological. Reflecting on unmet needs can provide insights into the true source of the conflict.

2. Values Clarification:

Identify the core values you felt were being challenged or compromised in a recent disagreement. List these values and reflect on why they are important to you. Understanding the role of differing values can help pinpoint the deeper issues driving the conflict.

3. Communication Analysis:

Revisit a past conflict and analyze the communication patterns that contributed to the escalation. Consider questions like, "Were there misunderstandings that fueled the disagreement?" and "How did the way we communicated affect the outcome?" This analysis can reveal how communication breakdowns serve as a source of conflict.

4. Empathy Mapping

Try to map out the conflict from the other person's perspective. List their possible unmet needs, values at stake, and perceptions of the communication breakdown. This exercise in empathy can help you see the conflict through their eyes, fostering understanding and compassion.

5. Conflict Journaling:

Keep a journal of conflicts, noting their sources, the emotions involved, and the resolution (if any). Over time, patterns may emerge that highlight recurring sources of conflict, offering valuable insights for personal growth and relationship improvement.

Communication Strategies for Conflict Resolution

By employing specific communication techniques tailored to conflict resolution, individuals can develop the skills necessary to approach conflicts with understanding, confidence and empathy. These techniques not only facilitate resolution but also contribute to the growth and strengthening of relationships, transforming conflicts from sources of stress into opportunities for deeper understanding and connection; within a safe and controlled environment.

Essential Communication Techniques for Conflict Resolution

Active Listening:

Active listening involves fully concentrating on what is being said rather than passively hearing the speaker's words. It means listening with all senses — paying close attention to the other person's words, tone of voice, body language, and even what is left unsaid. This technique helps in understanding the other person's perspective and demonstrates empathy and respect.

"I" Statements:

"I" statements are a way of expressing your feelings and needs without blaming or accusing the other person. This approach fosters open and honest communication. For example, instead of saying "You never listen to me," you could say, "I feel unheard when my suggestions are overlooked."

Clear Expression of Needs and Feelings:

Clearly articulating your needs and feelings is vital in conflict resolution. It involves being honest and direct about what you are experiencing without hiding or downplaying your emotions. This transparency can help prevent misunderstandings and provide a clear pathway to resolution.

<u>Role-Playing Scenarios and Exercises</u>

1. Active Listening Exercise: Pair up with a partner and share a recent minor conflict or frustration you've experienced. The listener should practice active listening, focusing entirely on the speaker's message, then summarize what they've heard to ensure understanding.

➤ Swap roles and repeat the exercise.

2. "I" Statements Role-Play: Create scenarios that typically lead to conflict (e.g., feeling undervalued at work or dealing with unmet expectations in a relationship). Practice expressing your feelings and needs using "I" statements in these scenarios.

➤ Role-play both sides of the conversation, focusing on using "I" statements effectively.

3. Needs and Feelings Clarification Exercise: Individually, think of a recent conflict and write down the main needs and feelings you experienced but may not have expressed.

➤ Share these with a partner or in a group setting, discussing the impact of openly communicating these needs and feelings on potential conflict resolution.

4. Empathy Building through Role Reversal: In pairs, choose a conflict scenario and role-play each side of the disagreement. Then, switch roles and replay the scenario.

➤ This exercise helps participants understand and empathize with the other person's perspective, fostering a deeper appreciation for effective communication in resolving conflicts.

5. Feedback Loop: After each role-playing exercise, engage in

a feedback session where participants can discuss what they learned, how they felt, and identify areas for improvement in their communication techniques.

The Role of Empathy in Resolving Conflict

Empathy, the ability to understand and share the feelings of another, is a powerful tool in the resolution of conflicts. By prioritizing empathy and employing strategies to cultivate it during disagreements, individuals can navigate conflicts more constructively, and connect with the deeper emotional undercurrents of disagreements.

Empathy: Bridging Understanding in Conflicts

- Empathy allows us to see beyond the surface level of conflicts and grasp the motivations, fears, and vulnerabilities that drive the other person's behavior.

- Empathy not only facilitates resolution but also strengthens relationships by demonstrating care, respect, and a commitment to mutual understanding.

Tips for Cultivating Empathy During Disagreements

1. Active Listening:

Commit to fully listening to the other person without interrupting or planning your response while they are speaking. Active listening signals that you are genuinely interested in understanding their perspective, laying the groundwork for empathy.

2. Mindfulness Practices:

Engage in mindfulness to manage your own emotions during a conflict. By staying present and calm, you can better attune to the other person's feelings and needs. Techniques such as focused breathing or grounding exercises can help maintain emotional equilibrium.

3. Perspective-Taking Exercises:

Deliberately attempt to see the situation from the other

person's point of view. Ask yourself questions like, "What might be causing them to feel this way?" or "How would I feel in their position?" This exercise can help you break out of your own perspective and appreciate the complexity of their experience.

4. Validate Feelings:

Even if you disagree with the other person's stance, acknowledging their feelings can be profoundly empathetic. Validation can be as simple as saying, "I can see why you would feel upset about this," which does not imply agreement but recognizes their emotional experience.

5. Practice Patience:

Recognize that reaching understanding through empathy may take time. Be patient with yourself and the other person as you navigate the complexities of the conflict. Empathy is not about quick fixes but about building bridges of understanding that can lead to lasting resolutions.

<u>Cultivating Empathy as a Habit</u>

- Empathy in conflict resolution is most effective when it's cultivated as a habitual response.

  * This requires ongoing practice and a commitment to developing one's capacity for empathy even outside of conflict situations.

- Engaging regularly in exercises that foster empathy, such as volunteering, listening to diverse perspectives, and practicing compassion in daily interactions, can enhance your ability to employ empathy during disagreements.

Negotiating and Finding Common Ground

Negotiating and finding common ground in conflicts is a skill that enhances not only the resolution process but also the overall quality of relationships. Effective negotiation respects the needs of all involved and aims for outcomes that all parties can accept, even if it requires compromise.

Principles of Effective Negotiation

Before entering a negotiation, understand your own needs and the desired outcome, but also consider the other party's perspective. Identify your non-negotiables and areas where you're willing to compromise.

- Self-Reflection: Write down your main goals and the reasons they are important to you.

    * This will help you stay focused during the negotiation.

- Understanding Flexibility: Determine aspects of your position where you can make concessions, and where you can't.

    * Having clear boundaries can facilitate smoother negotiations.

- Empathetic Perspective Taking: Try to understand the other person's needs and expectations. Think about <u>why</u> they might hold their views.

    * This empathy will not only help in crafting a more appealing offer but also in fostering goodwill.

Begin the negotiation by clearly stating your understanding of the conflict and your desired outcomes. Encourage the other person to do the same, ensuring that both sides are heard and understood from the outset.

Invest time in actively listening to the other person's needs and concerns. Understanding their perspective, can reveal creative solutions that might not have been apparent initially.

<u>Strategies for Compromise and Collaboration</u>

1. Identify Shared Goals:

   Start by identifying any shared goals or common interests. Focusing on these shared objectives can create a foundation of agreement, making it easier to navigate more contentious issues.

2. Brainstorming Solutions Together:

   Engage in joint brainstorming sessions where all parties can suggest potential solutions without criticism. This open, creative dialogue encourages collaboration and can lead to innovative solutions that satisfy everyone's needs.

3. Offer Options Rather Than Ultimatums:

   Present multiple options for resolving the conflict, rather than a single take-it-or-leave-it solution. Offering choices shows flexibility and a willingness to work together for a mutually beneficial outcome.

4. Be Willing to Give to Get:

   Recognize that compromise often means both sides may need to concede something. Approach negotiations with the mindset of finding a balanced solution, where each party feels they've gained more than they've lost.

5. Use "I" Statements in Negotiation:

   When discussing needs and proposing solutions, use "I" statements to express your perspective without placing blame. This can help maintain a positive tone and prevent defensive reactions.

6. Approach negotiations with a flexible mindset:

   Understanding that the final outcome may differ from your initial expectations and be open to outcomes that you may not have considered initially. Sometimes, the best solution is one that neither party had envisioned at the start of negotiations.

Healing and Rebuilding
After Conflict

The aftermath of a disagreement often leaves emotional wounds that need healing and a relationship that may require reinforcement. This is a process that requires time, patience, and intentional effort. By focusing on healing emotional wounds and reinforcing the relationship through positive interactions, it's possible to emerge from the aftermath of a disagreement stronger and more connected than before. Remember, the goal is not to erase the conflict but to grow from it, using the experience as a stepping stone towards a more understanding and resilient relationship.

Steps for Healing and Rebuilding

1. Recognize and acknowledge the emotional toll the conflict may have taken on everyone involved. Openly discussing feelings and experiences can help in understanding each other's emotional journey through the conflict.

2. Whether you were the cause of hurt or the one hurt, offering or seeking forgiveness can help in closing the emotional gap the conflict created. Remember, forgiveness is more about freeing oneself from lingering negativity than about absolving someone of their actions.

3. After a conflict, it's important to reaffirm your commitment to the relationship and to each other's well-being. This can be verbal or through actions that demonstrate your dedication to moving forward together.

Activities for Restoring Connection and Trust

Shared Reflection:

> Set aside time for a shared reflection session where both parties can discuss what they learned from the conflict and how they can prevent similar issues in the future.

This practice not only promotes understanding but also strengthens the relationship by focusing on growth and improvement.

Establish New Traditions:

Initiating new traditions can help in building fresh, positive memories. Whether it's a weekly coffee date, a monthly adventure, or a daily check-in, find something that allows you to spend quality time together, reinforcing your bond.

Acts of Kindness:

Engage in acts of kindness towards each other. These don't have to be grand gestures; even small acts can significantly impact how safe and valued each person feels in the relationship. Here are a few ideas:

- Personalized Gestures:

    Engaging in activities that the other person finds comforting or helpful. This could be taking on a task they dislike doing, cooking their favorite meal, or joining them in an activity they love but usually do alone.

- Handwritten Notes:

    Leave small notes of appreciation or encouragement for them to find. This can be a simple message left on the fridge, on a pillow, or in a book they are reading, expressing gratitude or admiration for something specific.

- Regular Check-Ins:

    Make a habit of checking in on how they are feeling about the relationship and what can be improved. This demonstrates your ongoing commitment to the relationship's health and your willingness to make adjustments as needed.

Professional Support:

Sometimes, healing and rebuilding after a conflict might

require professional support. Don't hesitate to seek help from a counselor or therapist, especially if the conflict has left deep emotional scars.

Preventing Unnecessary Conflict

While some conflicts are inevitable and can even be constructive, many arise from avoidable misunderstandings. By identifying common triggers and employing proactive strategies, it's possible to reduce the frequency and intensity of such conflicts. These proactive measures not only reduce the occurrence of conflict but also strengthen the foundation of trust and connectedness that supports healthy, resilient relationships.

Identifying Patterns and Triggers

➤ Take time to reflect on past conflicts, looking for common themes, situations, or behaviors that tend to precede disagreements. Identifying these patterns can provide valuable insights into triggers that can be addressed or avoided in the future.

➤ Personal triggers, such as specific words, tones of voice, or actions, can escalate emotions quickly. Recognizing your own triggers and those of others involved can help in managing responses and preventing unnecessary escalation.

➤ Factors, such as work stress, financial pressures, or health concerns, can increase susceptibility to conflict. Being aware of these stressors allows for more empathetic interactions and proactive stress management.

Strategies for Addressing Triggers Proactively

1. Open Communication:

Cultivate an environment where feelings, needs, and concerns can be openly discussed without fear of judgment or retaliation. Encourage honest and respectful communication about topics that could potentially lead to conflict.

2. Regular Check-Ins:

Establish regular check-ins to discuss relationship dynamics, individual needs, and any underlying issues that may be brewing. These check-ins can serve as a preventive measure against the build-up of resentment or misunderstanding.

3. Set Clear Boundaries:

Clearly defined boundaries help prevent conflicts by ensuring that everyone's needs and limits are respected. Discuss and agree upon these boundaries together, and commit to respecting them.

4. Practice Active Listening:

Active listening reinforces understanding and validation, reducing the likelihood of misunderstandings that can lead to conflict. Make a conscious effort to listen fully, reflect back what you've heard, and respond thoughtfully.

5. Develop Healthy Coping Strategies:

Equip yourself with healthy coping strategies for stress and emotional regulation. Practices such as mindfulness, exercise, or journaling can reduce the overall tension that might otherwise fuel conflicts.

6. Seek Constructive Feedback:

Encourage constructive feedback about how conflicts are handled and how communication can be improved. This openness to growth and change can significantly reduce the occurrence of unnecessary conflict.

Reflection and Action Steps

Understanding and navigating conflict is not just about resolution but about opportunities for personal growth and deeper connections. This section recaps practical steps derived from the chapter's guidance to empower you to apply these insights to real-life conflicts. Additionally, it offers journal prompts and reflection questions to encourage continuous personal development and improvement in conflict resolution skills.

<u>Practical Steps Recap</u>

➤Identify the Sources of Conflict: Begin by understanding the common triggers and underlying issues that lead to disagreements.

➤Employ Effective Communication Strategies: Utilize active listening, "I" statements, and clear expression of needs and feelings to foster constructive dialogues.

➤Leverage Empathy: Cultivate empathy to see conflicts from the other person's perspective, enhancing understanding and connection.

➤Negotiate and Find Common Ground: Approach negotiations with flexibility, seeking solutions that respect everyone's needs and promote mutual benefit.

➤Heal and Rebuild: After resolving a conflict, take steps to heal any emotional wounds and reinforce the relationship through positive interactions and rituals.

➤Prevent Unnecessary Conflict: Recognize and address patterns and triggers proactively through regular check-ins and open communication.

<u>Journal Prompts and Reflection Questions</u>

1. What patterns have I noticed in the conflicts I experience? How can I address these triggers proactively?

2. How do my communication habits contribute to conflicts? What steps can I take to improve my communication skills?

3. Recall a recent conflict. How could empathy have changed the outcome? How can I practice empathy more consistently in future disagreements?

4. Think about a time when a compromise led to a positive outcome. What did I learn from that experience about finding common ground?"

5. After resolving a conflict, what steps do I take to rebuild and strengthen the relationship? How can I make this process a regular part of my conflict resolution approach?"

6. What strategies can I implement to prevent unnecessary conflicts? How can regular check-ins and open communication be integrated into my relationships?"

Conclusion: Embracing Conflict as a Path to Connection

Identifying triggers and employing regular check-ins and open communication can mitigate many conflicts before they escalate, preserving the relationship's integrity. However, recognizing the common sources of conflict, including unmet needs, differing values, and communication breakdowns, is the first step in addressing disagreements constructively.

It's clear that our approach and mindset towards these inevitable challenges can significantly impact their outcomes. Techniques such as active listening, "I" statements, and clear expression of needs and feelings are crucial for resolving conflicts. When we stay flexible and keep a focus on mutual benefits, these techniques can lead to creative solutions that strengthen rather than weaken relationships allowing for resolutions that genuinely address the needs and feelings of all parties involved and cultivate empathy going forward.

The post-conflict phase is critical for healing emotional wounds and reinforcing the relationship through forgiveness, reaffirmation of commitment, and the establishment of new, positive interactions. As we continue on, let us carry the understanding that conflict, while challenging, is not something to be feared or avoided, rather it offers a unique pathway to deeper connection and intimacy.

CHAPTER 9: LETTING GO OF WHAT DOESN'T SERVE YOU

In the journey of personal development and emotional well-being, the concept of letting go stands as a cornerstone. Often misunderstood, letting go involves the deliberate and conscious decision to release memories, experiences, relationships, or habits that no longer serve our growth or happiness. This process is not about giving up or admitting defeat. Instead, it's about recognizing when something is no longer beneficial and choosing to release it to create space for new opportunities and experiences.

Letting go is an act of courage and self-compassion. It requires us to acknowledge the pain, disappointment, or stagnation certain aspects of our lives may cause and decide that we no longer wish to be defined or limited by them. This might include releasing grudges, past disappointments, unhealthy relationships, or self-limiting beliefs.

Understanding the difference between letting go and giving up is crucial. Giving Up often stems from frustration, despair, or defeat. It signifies an abandonment of hope or effort, sometimes prematurely, without fully exploring all possibilities or learning from the experience. Letting Go in contrast, letting go is a mindful and deliberate process. It comes from a place of strength and clarity, recognizing that holding on is more detrimental than beneficial. Letting go is about making room for growth, healing, and new possibilities.

Identifying What
to Let Go of

The journey toward personal growth and emotional well-being often requires us to shed elements of our lives that no longer serve our highest good. This can include habits, beliefs, relationships, and even long-held aspirations that have become counterproductive or harmful. Identifying what to let go of is a deeply personal and sometimes challenging process but this clarity is essential for making conscious choices that align with your values, goals, and the person you aspire to be, paving the way for a more fulfilling and authentic life.

<u>Strategies for Recognizing What to Let Go</u>

1. Assess Your Emotional Reactions:

    Notice which habits, beliefs, or relationships trigger negative emotional responses such as anxiety, frustration, or sadness. Persistent negative emotions can be indicators that something in your life is misaligned with your well-being.

2. Evaluate Your Energy Levels:

    Pay attention to how different aspects of your life affect your energy. Activities, thoughts, or people that consistently drain your energy rather than replenish it may need to be reassessed.

3. Reflect on Your Growth:

    Consider whether certain aspects of your life are contributing to your growth or holding you back. Elements that keep you stagnant or push you in a direction contrary to your desired path of growth are candidates for letting go.

<u>Exercises to Align with Values and Goals</u>

1. Values Clarification Exercise:

    Write down your core values and compare them to the various aspects of your life. Identify any discrepancies between what you value and your current reality. This exercise can highlight areas where change is needed.

2. Goal Alignment Reflection:

List your short-term and long-term goals, then assess which habits, beliefs, and relationships support these goals and which detract from them. This reflection can clarify what no longer serves your journey toward these aspirations.

4. Energy Inventory:

For one week, keep a diary of your daily activities, interactions, and thoughts, noting how each entry makes you feel energetically. Review your diary at the end of the week to identify patterns of energy gain or loss and consider changes based on this inventory.

5. Letting Go Letter:

Write a letter to yourself about what you need to let go of. This might include forgiving yourself for past mistakes, releasing a relationship that has ended, or changing self-limiting beliefs. The act of writing can be a powerful tool for acknowledging the need to let go and beginning the process.

The Emotional Challenges
of Letting Go

Letting go is a necessary step toward growth and healing, but it often brings emotional challenges like fear, guilt, and grief. Navigating these emotions is crucial for moving forward. This section explores the emotional difficulties of letting go and offers tips for managing them through self-compassion and seeking support. Remember, letting go isn't about erasing the past but making space for new possibilities and experiences that align with who you are becoming.

<u>Navigating Fear/ Fear of the Unknown:</u>
Letting go often means stepping into the unknown, which can be frightening. Fear of change, fear of making a mistake, or fear of regret can paralyze action.

<u>Tips for Managing Fear:</u>

1. Acknowledge Your Fear: Recognize and accept your fear as a natural part of the process.

2. Reframe the Narrative: Shift your perspective to view change as an opportunity for growth and new experiences.

3. Take Small Steps: Break down the process of letting go into manageable steps to reduce overwhelm.

<u>Dealing with Guilt/ Guilt over Leaving or Changing:</u>
Feelings of guilt may arise when letting go involves moving away from people, places, or roles that once defined us. This guilt can stem from perceived obligations or the fear of disappointing others.

<u>Tips for Managing Guilt:</u>

1. Understand the Source: Reflect on why you feel guilty and whether it aligns with your true values and needs.

2. Practice Self-forgiveness: Remind yourself that choosing your well-being is not an act of selfishness but of self-respect.

3. Communicate Your Needs: Openly discussing your reasons

for change can alleviate feelings of guilt and help others understand your perspective.

Processing Grief/ Grieving Loss:
Letting go of something significant, whether it's a relationship, a dream, or a part of your identity, involves a process of grieving. Acknowledging this grief is essential for healing.

Tips for Processing Grief:

1. Allow Yourself to Feel: Give yourself permission to experience the full range of emotions associated with your loss.

2.Seek Support: Lean on friends, family, or professional counselors to help you through the grieving process.

3. Find Expressive Outlets: Creative activities like writing, art, or music can provide a therapeutic outlet for your emotions.

** Be kind and patient with yourself as you navigate the complexities of letting go. Understand that it's a process, and it's okay to have moments of doubt or sadness.*

Practical Steps for
Letting Go

Letting go, while emotionally complex, can be navigated through a structured approach that facilitates decision-making, action, and closure. Letting go requires courage, reflection, and action, but by following these steps, you can navigate the path with grace and open yourself to new possibilities. Remember, letting go is not an end but a beginning, a vital step toward embracing the fullness of life and your potential within it.

<u>Step-by-Step Approach to Letting Go</u>
1. Acknowledge the Need to Let Go:

    Begin by recognizing what it is you need to release. This could be a relationship, a self-limiting belief, a past hurt, or an unattainable dream. Acknowledgment is the first step toward action.

2. Understand the Impact:

    Reflect on how holding on affects your emotional well-being and life. Consider the benefits of letting go and how it could open up new opportunities for happiness and growth.

3. Make a Decision:

    Decide firmly that you are ready to let go. This decision may require time and contemplation but is crucial for moving forward.

4. Plan Your Action:

    Determine what actions will symbolize or facilitate letting go. This could involve physical actions like removing reminders from your environment or more symbolic gestures.

<u>Techniques for Creating Closure</u>

1. Write a letter to the person, situation, or aspect of yourself you're letting go of. Express all your feelings, regrets, gratitude, and wishes.

* This exercise provides an outlet for your emotions and helps in processing them. There's no need to send the letter; the act of writing it is for your healing.

2. Create a personal ritual to mark the act of letting go. This could be as simple as lighting a candle and saying a few words of farewell, or as elaborate as a symbolic cleansing ceremony.

* Rituals can provide a tangible sense of closure.

3. Engage in mindfulness exercises focused on letting go. Visualize releasing the object of your attachment with each exhale, imagining it drifting away and dissolving. Concentrate on the sensation of lightness and relief with each inhale.

4. Talk to friends, family, or a therapist about your decision to let go.

* Sharing your journey can provide comfort, validation, and additional perspectives.

* After taking action, reflect on how you feel. It's normal to experience a range of emotions. Allow yourself time to adjust and heal. If feelings of attachment resurface, gently remind yourself of your reasons for letting go and the positive changes it brings to your life.

The Role of Forgiveness

Forgiveness is crucial in the art of letting go, acting as a powerful tool for emotional release and healing. It involves releasing resentment, anger, and bitterness toward oneself or others, paving the way for peace, closure, and growth. Forgiveness is a personal process that requires patience, compassion, and repeated commitment. By embracing forgiveness, you open yourself to healing, peace, and renewal, setting the stage for a life filled with joy, freedom, and meaningful connections.

Understanding Forgiveness

Forgiveness is not about condoning hurtful actions or denying the pain they've caused. Instead, it's about choosing to release the hold that this pain has on your life. Forgiving oneself and others can liberate you from the weight of past grievances, allowing emotional wounds to heal and enabling you to embrace the present and future with open-heartedness and clarity.

> ** Self-forgiveness is often the first step in the journey of letting go. Holding onto self-directed anger or disappointment can be a significant barrier to personal development and happiness.*

Reflective Journaling:

Write about a situation you find hard to forgive yourself for. Explore the reasons behind your actions and consider what you've learned since. Acknowledge your growth and the efforts you've made to change.

Self-Compassion Meditation:

Engage in meditations focused on self-compassion. Visualize offering kindness and understanding to yourself, acknowledging your humanity, and recognizing that mistakes are part of growth.

The Process of Forgiving Others

Forgiving others can sometimes feel insurmountable, especially when deep hurt is involved. However, forgiveness is a gift you give yourself—a release from the bitterness that can poison your well-being.

Empathy Practice:

Try to see the situation from the other person's perspective. This doesn't justify their actions but can help you understand their motivations, making forgiveness easier.

Letter of Forgiveness:

Write a letter of forgiveness to the person who hurt you. Like the letters mentioned earlier, there's no need to send it. This exercise is for your healing, helping you articulate and release your feelings.

Understanding Forgiveness's Role in Healing and Moving Forward

Forgiveness, both of oneself and others, is essential for truly letting go. It allows you to close chapters that keep you anchored to the past and opens up space for new experiences and relationships free from the shadows of resentment.

Emotional Relief:

Forgiveness can lead to profound emotional relief, reducing stress, anxiety, and depression.

Physical Health:

Letting go of long-held grudges through forgiveness has been linked to improved physical health, including lower blood pressure and a reduced risk of chronic illness.

Embracing Change and New Beginnings

Letting go creates space in our lives that can be filled with new experiences and discoveries. It's a liberating act that removes the barriers to growth and enables us to move forward with less baggage and more freedom. By releasing what no longer serves us, we make room for what truly aligns with our current selves and our future aspirations.

<u>Strategies for Embracing Change</u>

1. Setting Intentions:

   Begin by setting clear intentions for what you want to invite into your life. Intentions act as guiding lights, helping to focus your energy and actions toward the outcomes you desire. They can relate to personal development, career goals, relationships, or any other area of life where you seek growth.

2. Visualizing Future Possibilities:

   Visualization is a powerful tool for embracing change. Spend time regularly imagining your life as you wish it to be, including the new opportunities and experiences you want to attract. Visualization not only enhances motivation but also helps to solidify your intentions in your subconscious, making them more likely to manifest.

3. Cultivating Openness:

   Approach change with an open mind and heart. Being open to the unknown and willing to step out of your comfort zone are crucial for growth. Embrace the mindset that every experience, whether positive or negative, brings valuable lessons and opportunities for development.

4. Building Resilience:

   Change can be challenging, and not every attempt at something new will result in success. Building resilience helps you to navigate setbacks with grace, learning from each experience and remaining committed to your path despite obstacles.

5. Celebrating Small Wins:

Recognize and celebrate the small victories along the way. Acknowledging progress, no matter how minor, can boost your confidence and keep you motivated toward larger goals.

6. Seeking Support:

Surround yourself with a supportive community that encourages your growth and welcomes the new you. Having a network of friends, family, or mentors who support your journey can provide comfort and guidance as you navigate change.

Reflection and Action Steps

Deciding to let go and embrace new beginnings is a significant first step, but maintaining momentum is crucial for lasting change. By implementing these strategies, you can stay on your path, celebrate growth, and handle challenges with grace. Remember, every step forward, no matter how small, is a victory in your journey of personal transformation and renewal.

<u>Staying Committed to Letting Go</u>

1. Regularly Review Your Intentions:

   Keep your intentions and reasons for letting go at the forefront of your mind. Regularly review them to remind yourself why you started this journey and what you hope to achieve. This can help maintain your focus and motivation.

2. Track Your Progress:

   Create a system to track your progress in letting go and moving forward. This could be a journal, a checklist, or a visual representation like a progress bar. Seeing how far you've come can be a powerful motivator to keep going.

3. Celebrate Milestones:

   Recognize and celebrate each step you take away from what you've let go of and towards your new beginnings. Celebrating milestones, no matter how small, reinforces your achievements and boosts your morale.

<u>Navigating Setbacks and Doubts</u>

1. Expect and Accept Setbacks:

   Understand that setbacks are a natural part of any journey of change. Accepting that there will be ups and downs helps prepare you to face them with resilience rather than viewing them as failures. When you encounter a setback or find yourself doubting your decision, take time to reflect on what led to this moment. Use it as an opportunity to learn and adjust your approach if necessary.

2. Leverage Your Support System:

Don't hesitate to lean on your support system during challenging times. Friends, family, or a professional can offer perspective, encouragement, and advice to help you get back on track.

3. Practice Self-Compassion and Reaffirm Your Commitment:

Be kind to yourself during moments of doubt or when facing setbacks. Practice self-compassion by speaking to yourself as you would to a friend in a similar situation, recognizing that progress is non-linear.

Use moments of doubt as opportunities to reaffirm your commitment to letting go and moving forward. Reminding yourself of your intentions and the benefits of your journey can help reignite your motivation.

4. Adjust Your Strategies if Needed:

If you find yourself repeatedly facing the same setbacks, consider whether a change in strategy might be needed. Being flexible and willing to adjust your approach is key to overcoming obstacles and continuing your progress.

Conclusion: The Freedom in Letting Go

The journey of letting go involves recognizing and navigating deep-seated emotions like fear, guilt, and grief. It's a deeply personal and sometimes challenging process, but by employing practical strategies and exercises, we can find clarity and make conscious choices that align with our values and goals.

Remember, forgiveness plays a crucial role in this journey, acting as a powerful tool for emotional release and healing. It allows us to release resentment, anger, and bitterness, paving the way for peace, closure, and personal growth. Cultivating forgiveness is essential for moving forward and embracing a life filled with joy, freedom, and meaningful connections.

Maintaining momentum is crucial for lasting change. By tracking progress, celebrating milestones, and navigating setbacks with resilience, we can stay committed to our path. Every step forward, no matter how small, is a victory in the journey of personal transformation and renewal.

Letting go is not a one-time event but an ongoing practice that enhances our resilience, authenticity, and joy. It allows us to create space for new possibilities and experiences that align more closely with who we are becoming. Embrace the liberation that comes from letting go and welcome the endless possibilities that await you. As you continue on this journey, remember that each step you take brings you closer to a more fulfilling and authentic life.

Part 4:
Living a Life of Gratitude

CHAPTER 10: EMBRACING THE JOURNEY

Embracing gratitude as a lifelong practice shapes our perspectives, influences our actions, and guides our interactions. As we navigate different life stages, our focus of gratitude changes—from material possessions and achievements to relationships, experiences, and inner peace.

The understanding of gratitude's power deepens as we delve further into the practice, with anecdotes showing how it provides strength in adversity and amplifies joy in good times. The journey of gratitude includes challenges that lead to profound revelations, renewing our commitment and appreciation for the practice.

Gratitude requires adaptation and flexibility, as what works at one point may not be effective later. Living a life of gratitude is a personal and evolving path offering endless opportunities for growth, connection, and joy. Embrace the changes and challenges of this journey, knowing that each step in gratitude brings us closer to a fuller, more meaningful life.

Celebrating Your Progress

Recognizing and celebrating your progress is crucial for sustaining motivation and acknowledging positive shifts in perspective and well-being. The journey of integrating gratitude into your life brings growth, transformation, and a deeper awareness of abundance. Reflecting on these changes and celebrating milestones not only rewards your efforts but also affirms the value of gratitude, motivating you to continue.

Reflecting on Your Gratitude Journey

Notice the Small Changes:

Begin by reflecting on the subtle shifts in your daily life. Perhaps you find joy in moments you previously overlooked, or you've become more resilient in the face of challenges. Small changes often precede more significant transformations and are worth acknowledging.

Recognize Improved Relationships:

Consider how your gratitude practice has affected your relationships. You might find that expressing appreciation has deepened your connections or that you've become more empathetic and understanding toward others.

Acknowledge Enhanced Well-being:

Reflect on any improvements in your emotional or physical well-being since starting your gratitude practice. Many people report feeling happier, less stressed, and more content with their lives.

Celebrating Your Progress

Journaling:

Dedicate time to journal about your gratitude journey, highlighting specific instances where your practice has made a positive impact. This can serve as a powerful reminder of how far you've come.

Sharing Your Story:

Consider sharing your gratitude journey with friends, family, or even through social media. Sharing not only allows you to celebrate your progress but can also inspire others to embark on their gratitude journey.

Gratitude Gathering:

Host a small gathering or a virtual meet-up with close friends or fellow gratitude practitioners to share stories and celebrate your progress together. This can create a supportive community atmosphere that encourages continued practice.

Create a Gratitude Collage:

Compile images, quotes, and any other items that represent your gratitude journey into a collage. This visual representation can serve as a daily reminder of the progress you've made and the positive aspects of your life.

Set New Goals:

While celebrating your progress, consider setting new goals for your gratitude practice. Reflect on what aspects you'd like to deepen or expand, ensuring your practice continues to grow with you.

Encountering and Overcoming Challenges

Embarking on a journey of personal growth, like cultivating a gratitude practice, comes with challenges and setbacks. These obstacles are not signs of failure but essential parts of growth, offering lessons and opportunities for resilience. By adopting flexible strategies and maintaining a compassionate approach, you can navigate these hurdles and continue to cultivate a life enriched by gratitude.

Acknowledging Challenges

Recognizing Setbacks as Growth Opportunities:

Understanding that setbacks are natural and expected in any journey of personal development is crucial. Rather than viewing these obstacles as failures, see them as opportunities to deepen your practice and understanding of gratitude.

Accepting Fluctuations in Motivation:

It's normal for your motivation to ebb and flow over time. Recognizing this can help you be more compassionate towards yourself during periods of lower motivation and find ways to reignite your passion for the practice.

Strategies for Maintaining Gratitude During Difficult Times

Adjusting Expectations:

Be realistic about what you can achieve, especially during challenging periods. Adjusting your expectations doesn't mean lowering your standards but rather giving yourself grace and space to navigate obstacles with flexibility.

Finding New Ways to Connect with Gratitude:

When traditional gratitude practices seem challenging or stale, explore new methods that might reignite your interest. This could mean shifting from written journals to verbal expressions of gratitude or finding creative outlets to express thankfulness.

Focusing on Small Joys:

During difficult times, the grander aspects of life we are typically grateful for may seem distant. Shift your focus to the smaller, everyday joys and comforts, which can be more relatable and accessible sources of gratitude.

Seeking Support:

Don't hesitate to reach out to friends, family, or a community of like-minded individuals who can offer support, understanding, and perhaps share their strategies for overcoming similar challenges.

Practicing Self-Compassion:

Be kind to yourself and recognize that perfection is not the goal; the willingness to continue despite setbacks is a significant part of the journey. Practicing self-compassion can itself be an act of gratitude towards oneself.

Reconnecting with Your Why:

Remind yourself why you started this gratitude journey and the benefits you've noticed in your life since. Reconnecting with your initial motivations can provide a renewed sense of purpose and direction.

Incorporating Mindfulness:

Use mindfulness practices to stay present and find gratitude in the moment, even amidst challenges. This can help reduce overwhelm and reframe your perspective to one of appreciation.

Replacing F*ck It with
"Thank you!"

Recognizing the lessons and growth that come from hardships deepens our appreciation for life's journey. By embracing gratitude during tough times, in moments when we want to throw our hands up and say "f*ck It," staying and struggling through builds new strength. For every hardship, there comes a new lesson that moves us forward.

<u>Finding Gratitude in Life's Little Messes</u>

Reflect on Challenges:

Consider the tough times you've faced in the past and how they've shaped you. Reflect on moments where adversity led to personal growth, deeper relationships, or newfound strengths.

Identify Core Lessons:

Think about the key lessons learned from your experiences. These might include patience, resilience, empathy, or adaptability. Recognizing these lessons helps you appreciate the value in each challenge.

Embrace the Process:

Understand that growth often comes through struggle. Accepting this process can help you find gratitude even in the midst of difficult times.

Celebrate Small Victories:

Acknowledge the small successes and progress made along the way. Celebrating these moments reinforces the positive aspects of your journey.

<u>In-the-Moment Gratitude Activity: From "F*ck It" to "Thank You"</u>

Step 1: Pause and Breathe

- When you feel overwhelmed, stop whatever you're doing.
- Take three deep breaths, inhaling deeply through your

nose and exhaling slowly through your mouth.

* This helps calm your mind and bring you back to the present moment.

Step 2: Identify the Trigger

- Acknowledge what specifically is making you feel this way. Is it a person, a situation, or an unexpected challenge?

* Naming the trigger helps you gain control over your emotions rather than being controlled by them.

Step 3: Shift Your Focus

- Find one positive aspect or lesson within the challenge. Even if it seems small or insignificant.

* Identifying something positive helps shift your mindset.

- Ask yourself: *"What can I learn from this?"* or *"How can this help me grow?"*

Step 4: Express Gratitude

- Silently or out loud, say *"Thank you"* for the identified positive aspect or lesson.

* For example, *"Thank you for showing me that this path doesn't align with who I am,"* or *"I am grateful for this opportunity to grow"*

Step 5: Take a Positive Action

- Do one small positive action to reinforce your shift from *"F*ck it"* to *"Thank you."*

* This could be as simple as writing down your gratitude, sending a kind message to someone, or taking a short walk to clear your mind.

Reflection

As we conclude our exploration of gratitude's transformative power, it's essential to integrate its lessons into our daily lives. Reflect on how to deepen gratitude in various aspects of life and encourage its practice within your circles. Remember, the journey of gratitude is ongoing, with each day offering new opportunities to recognize and celebrate life's abundance.

<u>Reflective Prompts</u>

1. What are the most significant insights about gratitude I've gained from this journey

2. How has my understanding of gratitude changed or deepened?

3. In what ways have I noticed gratitude impacting my personal well-being and relationships?

4. What challenges have I faced in maintaining a gratitude practice, and how have I overcome them?

5. How can I inspire others to embrace gratitude in their lives?

6. What are specific moments or practices of gratitude that I want to incorporate more regularly into my daily routine?

7. Looking ahead, how do I envision my gratitude practice evolving? What steps can I take to foster this growth?

Thank you

It's clear that gratitude is more than a practice; it's a way of living. A life filled with gratitude acknowledges the full spectrum of human experience, embracing both highs and lows with a heart open to finding silver linings and lessons in every situation. This path, marked by challenges and triumphs, demonstrates the enduring power of gratitude to illuminate our lives and the world around us.

*When faced with life's messes and challenges, it's tempting to throw our hands up and say, "F*ck it." Instead, this book encourages you to take a deep breath and instead say "Thank you." Embrace life's ups and downs with a grateful heart, seeing them as opportunities for growth, connection, and happiness. Gratitude offers us a lens to view our lives and the world, not as obstacles to overcome but as a rich tapestry of experiences that shape, teach, and enrich us.*

As you continue on your journey, remember that gratitude is not just a destination to be reached but a path to be walked, a practice to be cultivated, and a gift to be shared. Let us each be a beacon of gratitude, lighting the way for ourselves and for one another, as we create a world transformed by the simple, profound act of giving thanks.

I hope this book is a milestone on your journey of gratitude. May it inspire you to carry forward the practices you've learned, share them with others, and continuously seek new ways to incorporate gratitude into your life. The ripple effect of your gratitude can spark a wave of positivity, kindness, and appreciation that transforms not just your life but also the lives of those around you and the world.

Thank you for embracing this journey. May the practice of gratitude continue to enrich your life in every possible way, today and always.